# SIZING DOWN

# Sizing Down

CHRONICLE OF A PLANT CLOSING

LOUISE MOSER ILLES

ILR PRESS AN IMPRINT OF

*Cornell University Press*

ITHACA AND LONDON

First published 1996 by Cornell University Press.
First printing, Cornell Paperbacks, 1997.

Printed in the United States of America

♾ The paper in this book meets the minimum requirements of the American National Standard for Information Sciences—Permanence of Paper for Printed Library Material, ANSI Z39.48-1984.

*Library of Congress Cataloging-in-Publication Data*

Illes, Louise Moser.
 Sizing down / Louise Moser Illes.
  p.  cm.
 "ILR"—CIP data sheet.
 Includes bibliographical references and index.
 ISBN 0-87546-351-7 (cloth: alk. paper)
 ISBN 0-8014-8434-0 (pbk.: alk. paper)
 1. Plant shutdowns—Utah—Orem—Case studies. 2. Downsizing of organizations—Utah—Orem—Case studies. I. Title.
HD5708.55U620745  1996
338.6'042—dc20                                    95-37620

Cloth printing     10   9   8   7   6   5   4   3   2   1

Paperback printing     10   9   8   7   6   5   4   3   2   1

# Contents

# Preface

It started out as a seminormal morning. It soon became clear, however, that everything that needed to be completed had already been done. There was not much left to do around the plant. Most of us were biding our time, waiting for that final exit process that would sever the ties for good.

People stopped by to give their best wishes and final goodbyes, which were inevitably stated as only temporary. "Let's stay in touch." "I'll give you a call and see how you are doing." Everyone fully recognized that this was not likely to happen. But maintaining these pretenses did help to soften the finality of leaving. All we could do was to swallow hard and wish other employees well—we were already missing the associations formed over so many years.

Over the past decade plant closures and downsizing have affected many different industries. The semiconductor industry in particular had been buffeted by the ups and downs of the computer market, foreign competition, technological breakthroughs leading to obsolescence, and the ever-increasing costs of the capital investments required to produce integrated circuits. Consequently, by the early 1990s many companies within the industry suffered from overcapacity and sought to find ways to counteract the high costs of doing business. Some companies tried to thwart this trend by forging business alliances with foreign firms. Others resorted to layoffs and plant closures to stem the flow of red ink.

In January 1992, managers of the semiconductor plant where I worked in Orem, Utah—Signetics—were notified that the plant would become the next victim of this troubled industry. Employees were informed that the plant would be closed in December of that year. The plant's work was carried out by long-term employees who had banked their careers on the company in Utah, and despite a full year's notice, most employees were unprepared to deal with the realities of finding new employment.

In my role as human resources manager I had been involved in processing many employee exits. After my own expedited interview and exit process, I gathered up what was left of my personal belongings and boxed-up materials, made arrangements for purchased office furniture, and prepared to take the final walk down the empty hallways. As I turned off the lights in my office for the last time, a lump lingered stubbornly in my throat as I gave my remaining coworkers a hug, knowing that I might never see them again.

Once I was outside, the world appeared strangely normal and unaffected. As I glanced back at the building that would soon be empty, it was as if the closing had all been a surrealistic dream. Why weren't there crowds of spectators outside watching the demise of a once very important business in the local community? Didn't they realize the significant impact this plant closure had had on so many lives? Perhaps even outsiders too had tired of the lengthy closure process. It was time to put it all behind us and move on. Yet something inside made us want to savor this moment and remember—something had happened to us that changed us. We were once a community of workers: sharing the daily travails of the business, making our singular contributions to the company, creating relationships that would soon transcend the organization. This was an experience that would live on for us—one we would never forget. We would never be the same again.

The idea for this book took shape after the closure was announced. I was no more prepared for the news than anyone else working at the plant. Early in February 1992, I attended a professional conference, where a colleague remarked that I should write a book about my experiences. We laughed about it at the time, but on further reflection, I considered the idea more seriously. After all, if in doing so I could find some release for my own anxieties and frustrations, why not? Such a book could make a real contribution to those who were in my position, a victim of downsizing and yet charged with its orchestration.

I immediately began keeping a journal to capture events as they unfolded. My entries made it quickly apparent that what I found most compelling were the stories of how individual employees responded to the closure process. Almost as intriguing was the way in which the parent company treated the plant over the course of that year. I found myself looking at the closure in a new way, no longer as an unwilling participant but as a critic who could advocate a better way of managing this pervasive phenomenon. This work is nonfiction. The stories actually happened, but I have changed the names of individuals in order to protect their identities.

The one-year closure period at Signetics offers the opportunity to analyze the phases that the employees and organizations go through during downsizing. I have organized this story as a monthly chronicle that attempts to capture each stage in a closure or major downsizing of a plant. The adaptive and adjustment process closely followed the experience of dealing with a family death or major illness. At each phase in a closure or downsizing, the potential for downward spirals is real, and yet the capability exists for moving quickly and successfully through the transition period.

In the final chapter I review the processes and interventions called for in successfully managing reductions-in-force or plant closures. I have highlighted key issues and made recommendations for management practices based on those that did or did not work well in this particular plant closure. In addition, at the end of each chapter there is a section analyzing the implications of that part of the story and providing practical suggestions and considerations by phase for employees, managers, and policymakers who are involved with the downsizing process or closure at a plant.

The events at Signetics have become a too-familiar scenerio for many employees in many different companies and industries. What challenges and problems face managers, policymakers, and employees who are forced into the circumstances of significant workforce reductions or plant closure? Can this process be understood and managed in such a way that both the company and the employees benefit in the end?

I hope that this story of individual employees, including managers, who were affected by the Signetics closure offers lessons to those who may someday find themselves dealing with plant closures or sizable reductions-in-force.

This work would not have been possible without my many friends and associates at the Signetics plant. It is to this community of former employees that I dedicate this book. My hope is that this account of our experiences will help provide support and guidance to those who find themselves in similar circumstances.

I want to thank my family for their encouragement and love. My appreciation to my husband for helping me get through this difficult time and for his unselfish devotion. To my children, Trevor, Alexander, and Lauren, I express my adoration and desire for a bright and promising future.

LOUISE MOSER ILLES

*Provo, Utah*

SIZING DOWN

# 1 Signetics and the Community

In 1966, Signetics—a small semiconductor company located in Sunnyvale, California—was searching for a stateside assembly facility to produce integrated circuits for its military customers. Provo, Utah, offered a low-cost, highly productive work force and access to a major university (Brigham Young University). The decision was made to build a small assembly operation in Utah to take advantage of this labor pool. Not long after the new assembly operation was staffed and running, a decline in the military market almost precipitated the closing of the Provo facility. But forces within the commercial business, which was desperate for increased wafer fabrication capacity, caused Signetics's management to turn their sights toward the Utah operation. In 1973 a new location just a few miles away in Orem was selected as a plant site to house both the small military assembly area and the new fabrication facility.

Orem is located in the heart of Utah Valley about forty miles south of Salt Lake City. This valley runs along the foot of the Wasatch Mountain range and encompasses twenty-one incorporated cities—the Provo-Orem combined metropolitan area having the largest population, around 270,000. The economy of the Provo-Orem area had been consistently growing. There was low unemployment there (around 4 percent) and a young, well-educated and highly skilled work force. Orem was attractive to new business and had also acquired the moniker of "Family City, USA," partly due to the high birth rate and number of families (40 percent of whose members were sixteen or younger), and partly to the strong Mormon influence on local culture.

The physical facility eventually grew to become a 520,000-square-foot building on twenty-three acres of land. The plant housed seven major areas, including two wafer fabrication facilities (which were combined in 1989), a circuit design group, the military assembly area, an electrical sort testing area, a product engineering group, military final test and distribution, and the administrative and support services area. More than half the employees worked in wafer fabrication. The work force was composed of around 65 percent nonexempt workers, 60 percent of whom were manufacturing operators and 40 percent clerical workers and technicians. Of the remaining 35 percent exempt personnel, 40 percent were engineers and technical people, and 60 percent were nontechnical white-collar workers. Complicating things further, changes in the corporate organization over the years had created three separate reporting structures during most of the plant's existence. Ensuing corporate political machinations in this reporting structure led to the demise of many an uninitiated manager not fully attuned to the existing plant culture. Unless each operations manager, including the plant manager, was sensitive to the implications of any single operational decision on the rest of the plant organization, there would be swift repercussions back through the other line operations as each manager communicated everything through his or her respective reporting structure. Those managers who only looked out for their own operation and disregarded the best interests of the plant would find themselves caught in the crossfire of the corporate divisions and eventually if not promptly relieved of their responsibilities.

In the high-tech semiconductor industry it was unusual to house both assembly and wafer fabrication operations together in one plant. With operations in wafer fabrication becoming more centralized in the company, the engineering process technology more complex, and the production environment requiring a more restricted, "cleanroom" standard, the two main manufacturing areas' problems and challenges appeared increasingly disparate and disconnected. The plant management team, however, recognized the benefits of a semiconductor plant with complete design-to-final-packaged-product capability, and they worked hard to maintain plant unity and exploit some of the unique advantages this complete integrated circuit processing structure offered for technical recruiting, employee career mobility, customer visits, quick product prototype production, and enhanced job training purposes.

Throughout the cycle of recession and boom in the industry, the Orem plant faced continual reductions-in-force and growth spurts that caused its employment level to vary from less than 100 employees in 1973 to a high of around 2000 in 1988. At its peak, the plant produced about 60 percent of the wafers and 70 percent of the die for the entire company and accounted for 50 percent of the sales dollars generated. In 1988, more than one billion die were produced at the plant at the lowest manufacturing costs, shortest cycle time, and highest productivity and quality levels in the company. Over the years, the plant had become a significant player in the local economy. It contributed more than $570,000 in property taxes, making Signetics the largest taxpayer in the city, and at one point, it provided more than $40 million in annual payroll.

At the time of the closure, the plant was the fourth-largest employer in the city of Orem (WordPerfect Corporation, which had more than four thousand employees, was the largest). Businesses throughout the county, including University Mall, the state's largest shopping mall, frequented by plant employees and located just across the street from the plant, felt the ripple effects of the closure. Fortunately, the local economy of Provo-Orem had a reputation as one of the fastest growing metropolitan areas in the country. The area had recently received a lot of national attention—in 1991 it was rated as *Money* magazine's best place to live in America. *Time* magazine had also recently done an article further promoting the image of "the nation's youngest, best educated and most productive work force." In addition, the region's driving economic force had switched from tourism (skiing, national parks) to "silicon," with the largest concentration of software companies in the nation and the third-greatest concentration of high-technology companies (230 high-tech businesses with total sales of $2.5 billion in 1993). The local economic development commission had worked hard to capitalize on the favorable business climate, which, ironically, began when the city was named after Walter C. Orem, a man who never actually resided in the city. He was the president of the Salt Lake and Utah Electric Interurban Railroad at the time, and the strategy was to use the name Orem so the community might receive some worthwhile favors from the railway promoter.

The up side of the Signetics plant closure was that it occurred during a time when the economy could provide opportunities for affected workers. The various manufacturing operations and businesses in the county's burgeoning software and health products industries absorbed many of the well-trained workers from the plant. By April 1993, most of the former plant employees had found new jobs, new careers, or they had decided to return to school. The down side of this affair was that it ever happened at all.

# 2 The Announcement

Anticipation was evident in the faces of the employees gathered in the rented auditorium. We all waited to hear the president of the company make his announcement. Over the last several days, speculation and rumor that a major announcement would be given had dominated lunch conversations, business meetings, and hallway discussions. The company president had cancelled his last regular quarterly visit and communication meeting. Our curiosity was piqued, and the rented auditorium was packed. Some believed that the fabrication production area would be shut down, while others assumed that the division would undergo major restructuring. But no one really expected to hear what came next.

First, the president welcomed the employees and thanked us for our attendance. He reiterated his commitment that he would provide first-hand delivery of information that affected us. Then he read the following text:

> The decision has been taken to close our 3"/4" bipolar fabrication operations (fab 21) and all related support including the military assembly and test activities in Utah by the end of 1992. The Utah plant has been an outstanding operation for over twenty-five years but has reached the end of its effective life. All processes necessary to our continuing product portfolio will be transferred to other company fabs over the balance of 1992.

The company president proceeded to announce the details of timing and transferring of the operations to other company sites. Only a few of us listened to the rest of the announcement; rather we glanced around, trying to absorb the shock of those words. One employee raced down the aisle toward the exit to try to salvage an outside job offer he had recently turned down. Husbands and wives and co-workers sitting together turned to one another in mutual disbelief. A short question-and-answer period followed, but it was evident that details would not be forthcoming. Many employees were too stunned, too overwhelmed, to ask questions.

As we slowly made our way back to our various work stations and offices, we said little. Groups formed in corridors as coworkers shared the message with those who had not attended the meeting. One hallway conversation summarized the situation: "I've been here fifteen years and a loyal employee all that time. This is the thanks we get." We all asked each other, "How can they do this to *our plant?*"

One twenty-five-year employee said, "It's like a death in the family. You are shocked at first, then you go through disbelief and denial that it could really be happening to you. Now I'm feeling angry at the company and those guys who made this decision to close down a place that I have devoted my career to."

Any productive work came virtually to a standstill that day. Slowly, employees began to trickle out of the plant and make their way home to confront with their families the reality of the plant closure. Black Wednesday, as we later referred to it, became the date from which everyone in the plant began to mark time.

Minutes after the closure announcement was made, the media got word of it. Reporters were attempting to verify their sources on the plant closure. Plant managers had already made plans to provide a press release to all the local media affiliates. The plant manager and visiting corporate representatives designated a coordinator to field media questions and release an official company statement. All attempts by the media to get interviews and tape footage inside the plant were rebuffed. Employees who had access to windows watched reporters and film crews position themselves outside to interview exiting employees. Many employees, as they left the plant, were happy to accommodate these efforts to get first-hand reactions to the closure.

The next day, we shared our reactions to the press coverage and traded impressions on how each news channel had reported the event. It was a day of excitement over the attention, nervousness from experiencing a major event in the local community, and relief in the final resolution of rumors that had been building during the past month. A sort of calm temporarily engulfed the plant. We felt somewhat liberated from the anxiety created by all the uncertainty of the past year.

The Utah plant had been the profit center for the company, even during its most unprofitable years. We had a reputation for being a hard-working, loyal, and stable work force. Over the past few years, many Utah plant employees resented the New Mexico plant for getting most of the attention and resources of the company. Indeed, an adversarial relationship had developed within some groups in the Utah plant who felt most threatened by the build-up occurring in the New Mexico plant.

It appeared that the decision to close the plant had been based on excess capacity, which the company had built up over the past few years in the wafer fabrication operation. The New Mexico fabs were state-of-the-art, clean-room facilities and had ended up with the company's newest proprietary fabrication process. Several of the engineers had fought bitterly over the decision to move the new fab process to New Mexico instead of Utah. They foresaw that if the Utah plant did not get the new process, no new fab areas would be built in the plant. In fact, many of the engineers had given up other career opportunities to stay in Utah, banking on the hope that some day the Orem plant's empty fab shell added in 1988 in anticipation of needed capacity would become the company's next high-tech fab operation.

Some employees speculated that the demise of the Utah plant could be traced back five to six years, when one particularly aggressive vice president—with a vision and a hidden agenda—had advocated pursuing microprocessors and MOS (metal oxide semiconductor) technology beyond the market and company's manufacturing capability. The New Mexico plant became this vice president's obsession. The fab areas constructed there were built without a substantial product sales or marketing base. Other theories on the reasons behind the Utah plant's demise circulated. For employees with the greatest involvement in the events that transpired in New Mexico, most were convinced that the division vice presidents were caught in a power struggle and vying for control. The fab operations in Utah were producing wafers in the standard logic product areas. But this product line was generally perceived as a dying business to be replaced by the more complex MOS products. The local plant quickly became the "subtract answer" to the company's quest for profitability and new product competitiveness.

As we reflected on what we now knew, events of the previous year began to take on a new meaning. Early in 1991, some of the corporate organizational development (OD) specialists had visited the plant to interview a broad sample of employees. The purpose of the visit appeared to be a more in-depth follow-up to a company survey administered the previous year. Designed as an employee satisfaction feedback tool in the company's quest to apply for the Malcolm Baldridge Award, the survey results had revealed considerable concern from plant employees, especially about a developing morale problem in the plant and the poor treatment some employees felt they were receiving from local management. Previously, on one of his quarterly communication trips to the plant, the company president had told us that he was concerned about the survey results from the plant. He had also received a number of personal notes and messages from plant employees, containing negative comments, which he felt compelled to investigate.

Many of the senior plant employees expressed to the president and corporate staff their dissatisfaction with what they perceived as unresponsive management. A number of employees had made career decisions to stay in the Utah area; and since other job options in the local area were very limited, they stayed with the company. The stakes were high for these committed individuals, because they saw their destiny as linked to that of the company's. Joseph, one of these concerned employees, sent regular e-mail messages to the president about perceived local management transgressions. These perceived transgressions included such things as assigning employees long hours of overtime to meet production schedules and not responding to certain employee requests to be promoted or transferred. But Joseph soon admitted his true intention to coworkers: he wanted to see plant managers held responsible for their actions and, in some cases, relieved of their positions for what he viewed as incompetence. The president took this feedback to heart and wanted to investigate, which resulted in nothing less than an employee feeding frenzy. Not only those who had a legitimate concern were offering feedback; anyone who had a grievance with the company, however small, seized upon this opportunity to revisit his or her complaints.

During the week they surveyed the plant, the OD specialists were bombarded with comments, concerns, and complaints. Many of the plant employees began to form expectations: if enough people complained, there might actually be some changes that could benefit them individually and possibly the company as a whole. Well-intentioned employees had no idea their comments would cause the corporate staff to focus intensely on the plant and to perceive there was a malaise in the plant.

Not long after the plant survey visit in early 1991, certain individual managers in the plant began to have long, closed-door meetings with the visiting division vice president, to whom the plant managers now reported. Shortly thereafter, an announcement was made that several of the plant staff managers would be leaving to "pursue career interests elsewhere." The reverberations were significant—entire operations within the plant began to reorganize to absorb these management departures. As recruiting efforts for replacements began, interim corporate appointees were assigned to manage affected functions. One employee who had participated in the survey meetings and voiced concerns summed up employee reactions this way: "Sure, I was one of those who agreed with the comments made in my group that was surveyed. But who would have ever guessed it would come to this? If I had any idea that it would have resulted in those managers leaving, I would not have expressed my feelings so strongly. I wanted to see some things change around here, but not like this!"

A newly appointed division vice president to whom the plant managers reported began to make regular stays at the plant to manage the aftermath. He held communications meetings with us to convey his intent to create a climate that was more open and responsive to our "concerns." He invited all the employees who had concerns or grievances to set up appointments with him to discuss issues. It wasn't long before lines began forming at his office door whenever he was in town. Plant supervisors and managers began to feel undermined and bypassed, as they watched their employees take concerns to the vice president rather than try first to work out these problems locally. When human resources personnel were brought in to investigate the concerns, it became apparent that many of these employees were bringing up past issues that supposedly had been resolved earlier, but not to the satisfaction of the employee. Some plant employees were forthright about their desire to see their managers or supervisors get into trouble with the company. In the end, not much changed from the status quo, since the solutions to the problems were virtually the same ones employees had already received from their supervisors or manager. A new climate of fear and reprisal, coupled with a general distrust between employees and their supervisors, now dominated the plant. Managers and supervisors were left feeling disenfranchised.

Rumors that the vice president was overcommitting to the employees and would be unable to deliver on his *alleged* promises began to grow. When little changed in the plant, aside from some managers leaving and employees' expectations rising, the vice president's effectiveness was questioned. More profoundly, the engineers in the plant were disturbed by his lack of depth of understanding of the technical issues surrounding the division's products. This vice president proved unable to provide the necessary leadership to make significant headway in stemming the red ink that continued to flow from the division. The single greatest frustration among the plant technical workers was the lack of a consistent product strategy for the division; there was no consensus-building to form a united front to customers and within the company. Not only did the vice president fail to make headway in dealing with these problems, he was adding to the fracas by making side commitments to each group that everyone knew were unlikely to be fulfilled. Less than a year into this vice president's tenure, corporate officers announced that a new vice president had been appointed and that the incumbent would be "pursuing other interests." Later, in a conversation I had with a local manager who had been ousted by the outgoing vice president, it became clear that this same vice president had been in discussions with the president and parent company to close the Utah plant almost one year before the actual announcement.

# 3   January
## The Initial Shock

Late in January it was strange to review the 1992 plant objectives, written the first part of the month. Everything had taken on a new perspective, and those objectives now seemed foreign and superfluous. Obviously, planning would take on a whole new meaning as we prepared for the closure in the coming year. Why bother to plan at all, when each day would undoubtedly bring new information and changes that would make previous plans obsolete and planning an exercise in futility? It took real effort to look forward instead of backward. At this point, the only question that seemed worthwhile was How current is my résumé? We would need to make or regenerate contacts to stimulate new job opportunities. We all wondered what the best strategy would be: wait until after the initial wave of résumés hit local businesses or try to beat the rush by being one of the first? All those wanting to stay in the area would no doubt satisfy the major employers' needs in a matter of days. There was some comfort in action. Just getting the reemployment process going provided a sense of progress.

## First Reactions

Each day was a roller coaster ride of emotions about the impending closure. It was tough not to worry about the future. It seemed that everyone wanted to know immediately what everyone else was doing or planning and where they were applying. If you didn't have answers, you started to feel guilty or irresponsible for your lack of planning. Yet some were a bit more relaxed and self-composed about their unknown future. This enabled others to allow themselves this same luxury—after all, at this juncture, December seemed a long way away.

Nevertheless, almost everyone had had a few sleepless nights. Telling yourself that this was a natural process helped to a degree, but the anxiety was real and relentless. Facing the family with answers about your plans was even more stressful. You wanted to reassure them that you would survive and so would they and all would be well, but you also needed to seek solace and comfort by sharing your personal fears and anxieties with them.

Employee responses to the closure news emerged in some interesting patterns. Those in dual-income families seemed to be weathering the storm with less stress than others. Low company seniority also appeared to help cushion the blow. While family size didn't seem to make much difference in stress levels, upper-income employees seemed to have more difficulty coping than those with middle or lower incomes. Maintaining a certain standard of living was unquestionably a key concern to those with higher incomes. Utah was not known for high wages; career changes would be inevitable for many who wished to stay in the area.

## Planning for Retraining

When the announcement was made, the plant had just initiated a communication training program, the first of several planned interventions to create a more open and effective plant culture. The plant training council had recently been reactivated to lead these training efforts. But the training council now faced having to scrap the new program and refocus their efforts. Instead of molding a new culture, they were forced to maintain the existing one in the face of discouragement, inertia, and general animosity. Consequently, the training council initiated a needs assessment to ascertain what retraining programs would now help to prepare employees to find other employment.

Earlier, the company had pledged support to provide funds for outplacement and retraining. Additionally, the governor's office had promised assistance in finding state monies for the retraining effort. Ironically, just months ago, the plant had acquired substantial state funding to "revitalize" and become more competitive in the industry as a manufacturing facility. The state approved a significant budget to fund extensive training efforts to upgrade the skill base of the employees. After the closure announcement, the state funding coordinators were reassured that the plant staff had had no knowledge of the plant closure when the funds were requested. Now the council hunkered down to the task of determining which revitalization training programs already had committed funds and which programs had not. The state funding agency reduced the company budget according to what had been spent, and then all efforts turned toward retraining. The process of trying to determine available funding for the employees' reemployment process began.

Shirley, an employee in human resources, had recently transferred to the Utah plant from the California headquarters. Having been in the plant for less than a year, she was caught off guard by the closure announcement. She and her husband had decided to relocate to Utah, where Shirley could continue to work for the company as she approached her retirement years. A very personable and outgoing individual, Shirley seemed to take the closure news in stride, more concerned about the impact of the closure on her coworkers than on her personally: "At least I don't have to worry about feeding a family, and my husband has retirement benefits through his company. Besides," she teased, "who would want to hire someone like me when they have all these younger candidates to choose from?" Even though she was fairly new to the plant, Shirley was known for her sense of humor and optimistic attitude. She quickly volunteered to help with the retraining and outplacement programs, so she could feel as if she were making a positive contribution in helping others make the adjustment.

## Implications

### Allow Time to Adjust

Once plant downsizing or closure is announced, employees need time to adjust to the initial shock. Employees with significant company tenure will likely be hit hardest. For these employees, the community of friends and coworkers in the plant may be an important source of personal security and identity. Over the years, coworkers can share confidences and develop deep friendships through work experiences. When faced with the loss of these relationships, employees may express profound sorrow. Along with the fear of reentering the job market—for some it may be only the second time—employees may feel panic and a sense of immobilization.

After the announcement, managers should provide employees some slack, allowing time to regroup. Employees should take the time to grieve over the loss of friendships and plant community, encouraging one another to talk openly about the reductions-in-force and the personal impact they will have. Those affected should not suppress the emotions and anger that inevitably will surface.

### Be Aware of Alternatives

Some employees may want to challenge company management about their consideration of other available options besides downsizing or closing the plant. There are creative alternatives to plant closure and downsizing, and these may apply (Schippani 1987). Those who will be in charge of formulating policy affecting plant downsizing or closure should be familiar with other options available to companies. One would hope that company officials have been aware of these options and considered their applicability before the decision has been made to downsize or close a plant. Be clear from the beginning about the reasons for a plant closure or major layoffs. Employees should expect management to have solid business reasons for closing a plant and will often demand to know all considerations in the decision-making process. Press releases will generally not be enough to satisfy the employees' .need to know. Employees will be distrustful and suspicious at the outset and may look for rationale other than what is provided. Although the reasons for the Utah plant closure were mainly capacity and technical obsolescence, most employees perceived the culminating factor to be malaise within the plant. They believed that the Utah plant no longer enjoyed the good will of senior management at corporate headquarters, which allowed those in power to move quickly without considering alternatives to closure.

Several Utah plant employees explored employee ownership as a legal means to keep it operating. Although a plan never emerged, the experience of working with top management and the local community to explore employee ownership proved to be an enabling experience for these employees.

### Satisfy Notification Requirements

If downsizing is unavoidable, companies should satisfy the legal requirement of sixty-days advance notice to employees (WARN Act). If more advance notice can be provided, it will benefit all involved, as we learned from the Utah plant closure experience. More notice helps to cushion the blow and more thoroughly prepare employees and managers for the process.

### Ask and Answer

Employees should ask policy and impact questions forcing those responsible to do the appropriate research. Managers need to respond honestly and forthrightly to these questions. Answers to policy and procedure questions may not come all at once, but these data can provide employees the necessary information to begin formulating contingency plans.

At the Utah plant, each employee found a different way to deal with the closure, but all sought reassurance that the company would in some way see them through that difficult period. Above all, employees did not want to feel abandoned and forgotten, to feel that once the decision was made, the company would move on to other issues. The first responses from the company to employee queries should be well-timed and sensitive. Even though answers may not be available initially, managers can outline some basic ground rules and guidelines that should include severance pay conditions and release date information. Policymakers should create a process through which employee questions can be noted, researched, and responded to expeditiously. Utah plant employee questions grew from a list of a dozen or so that arose during the initial communications meetings, to more than one hundred. This list of questions and their answers were grouped by topic and published as a document employees could use as a reference guide throughout the preclosure period (see Appendix 1.) Open forum discussions with employees, although uncomfortable at times, enable managers to keep the communication process going. Initially, weekly meetings may be necessary. As the issues and questions are addressed, however, biweekly and then monthly meetings should suffice.

*Plan Release Process*

One of the most pressing closure issues at the Utah plant was the timing of operation shutdowns and the subsequent release dates for individual employees. As later chapters make clear, this issue was not adequately addressed at the Utah plant and continued to be a cause of employee distress for several months. If managers can arrange to plan the shutdown schedule early with release date information, employees will know how long they can continue working and when they should begin the reemployment search process.

Referral services such as employee assistance plans, EAPs, allow employees who feel particularly vulnerable to seek counseling for themselves and their families. Policymakers should take measures to provide local management with the tools and autonomy to manage the details of the downsizing process. This necessarily includes an operations shutdown schedule and a severance and benefits package for all affected employees who remain until their release date. Familiarity with other plant downsizing or closure cases and "best practices" (U.S. Department of Labor 1990) will help to manage the process more successfully by avoiding major problems. Through establishing trust and confidence in local plant management and providing training in this process, the company will benefit from having more empowered managers who are closer to the needs of the plant.

*Refocus Training*

Downsizing causes immediate repercussions to ongoing training programs at the plant. If there is a plant training manager or coordinator, this individual must quickly refocus training efforts and resources to prepare employees for their impending outplacement. Often, state and local funding is available to finance retraining programs at affected plants. Generous government grants may more than cover the expenses for these programs, so these sources should be investigated.

The reduction-in-force experience will live on in the lives of every affected employee. Companies must not treat it as just another tough but necessary business decision. In the end, what will matter is that the company took time to try to address employees' needs. If employees remain productive until the end, the company will surely continue to value their contributions and work to meet those needs.

Stage 1: Initial Shock

| Employees | Managers | Policymakers |
|---|---|---|
| —Take time to grieve<br>—Challenge downsizing or closure assumptions<br>—Ask policy and impact questions<br>—Maintain productivity | —Hold open forum discussions with employees<br>—Respond honestly to questions<br>—Compile issues/concerns list<br>—Formulate release date plan to match operations shutdown | —Consider options to downsizing or closure<br>—Provide referral services<br>—Formulate severance/benefits package for employees<br>—Be familiar with plant downsizing and closure literature (best practices)<br>—Have an operations shutdown plan<br>—Establish trust and confidence in local plant management |

# 4 February
## Moving to Anger and Denial

Emotions were running high as the reality of the closure set in. Plant employees started to sort through the tangle of issues and dilemmas that faced them in their individual circumstances. The human resource group became the focal point of many of these issues and questions. It was painfully obvious that answers were needed. We held general communication meetings each shift to provide preliminary responses to questions and to make plans for next steps. Benefit issues such as medical insurance, the 401K program, and retirement options dominated the discussions. Existing policies appeared unforgiving under the circumstances, and employees were requesting exceptions for pension vesting, benefit coverage, and other contingencies (see Appendix 1).

### Employee Questions and Concerns

Some commonly asked questions included What happens if I decide to quit now or sometime before the end of my assignment? What do I get if I stay to the end of my assignment? When will the reduction-in-force begin? How many people will be relocated with the company elsewhere? Do we have specific shutdown schedules? Will there be early retirement incentives available? What outplacement and retraining support will be provided? Can we make changes to our benefits now?

The questions continued. Since many employees feared the company would do little or nothing to protect employee interests, the fact that the answers to many questions would require research caused employee speculation and anxiety. Battle lines were being drawn between those who were perceived to represent the interests of the company and those who sought to protect the best interests of the employees. Trust was eroding, particularly around the issues of severance pay and completion bonus eligibility.

The company would offer basic severance pay, which was required by policy, and an additional bonus was offered as an incentive for employees to stay until their completion dates. This amounted to double severence pay as a potential compensation package. Consequently, many plant employees wanted assurances that they would be eligible for this benefit, even if they left earlier for another job. Some were even negotiating their release dates to coordinate with possible job offers, without regard to the interests of their area or work group. It was not unusual to hear statements like "To hell with the company for what they did to me—I'll make sure I get out of here with everything I have coming to me." Meetings between local management and plant employees were noticeably tense, even hostile. Interestingly, few employees stopped to recognize the fact that the local management team faced the same set of prospects that they did. The plant management team appeared to be sincere in doing everything they could to negotiate the general interests of the plant employees with the corporate staff.

One event in February reinforced the corporate staff's lack of sensitivity to the plant employees' dilemma. An announcement came that unexpectedly good fourth-quarter profits would warrant a company celebration with ice cream sundaes for all and a gift give-away to be held in the cafeterias on all shifts at each site. This triggered immediate outrage from many of the Utah plant employees. How could the company expect us to celebrate something that is clearly irrelevant to us in the face of our plight? At best, this created perceptions of poor taste and bad timing. When local plant management picked up on this reaction (some of the managers had anticipated it and tried to get the announcement changed), an e-mail quickly modified the announcement: "Let's consider this as a celebration for our good efforts here in the plant and for all of the good times we have had together." This message did diffuse much of the anger, but many plant employees didn't bother to show up to the celebration.

The plant staff quickly formulated responses to some of the major issues and concerns that employees had raised. The human resources staff held another communication meeting to present the retraining and outplacement programs and provided a handout called "What To Expect."

1. We will not have all the answers to all the questions immediately, but will follow through in answering all questions.
2. Plans will be developed to phase down the facility beginning late third quarter.
3. Employees will be given a projected release date by their supervisor.
4. All employees will receive a minimum of 60 days written notice prior to their actual release date.
5. Plans will be developed to provide retraining to employees on computer skills and programming.
6. Outplacement training will be conducted, and plans are being developed to start up an in-house outplacement activity approximately midsummer.

This information successfully relieved most of the immediate pressure from plant employees for ready answers.

## Company Image and Rumor Control

Events in the local community were stirring considerable interest within the plant. A group composed of local community officials, including the mayor, was formed to investigate the possibilities of another business buying out the plant, along with the company's existing capital. This group also included some of the employees who wanted to stay in the area and retain their positions and skill base. Called SOS, the group modeled its efforts after a similar situation that had occurred in the community. Some years earlier, a local steel mill was shutting down and put several thousand jobs in jeopardy. Through the efforts of some local officials and organized labor, a buyer was found, and the plant was sold and reopened with a new owner. The steel mill reopening sparked a communitywide revitalization that reverberated through several local industries. The SOS group resolved to attempt another miracle by marketing the plant's assets.

It appeared that in the community the company's image was taking a real bruising. Several plant employees had written letters to the company president to get his blessing and support for the SOS efforts. Instead, they received a passive head nod with no real encouragement or financial support. After meeting with the company president, the SOS newsletter reported, "We recognize that the company's position to remove the wafer fab facility eliminates the hopes of finding a company to purchase the facility as is. It does not eliminate the possibility that a semiconductor firm may purchase the facility and capitalize on the existing labor force. For that option to occur, it will take a buyer with substantial financial backing."

Another community snafu occurred when a local news channel ran a story reporting the state's poor air quality. When efforts failed to get the current plant manager to corroborate that the air quality was one of the main reasons for the plant closure, the news crew contacted the former plant manager who was a bit of a local personality and had been very active with the economic development group and the governor's office. He confirmed the effects of the poor air quality in the community and on business.

That evening, a local channel reported that company officials had been allegedly influenced to expand operations in New Mexico rather than in the state because of the inferior quality of the air in Utah valley. The taped interview with the former plant manager seemed unequivocal, but after viewing the news report, both the current and former plant managers perceived the results as a misrepresentation—an instance of unethical journalism. They were both surprised to hear the report and disagreed with the final conclusions. The air quality in the valley had no bearing on the decision to close the plant. The former plant manager felt strongly that he had been quoted out of context. Both men later called the news station to complain and protest the media's coverage. Angry employees called the plant manager that day and throughout the week to inquire as to why the company had kept this important piece of information from them. The plant manager was forced to do a lot of explaining. Meanwhile, trust continued to erode between plant managers and the other employees.

Support Services

It is amazing how a plant closure announcement draws other businesses, like hungry predators circling around a fresh kill. The plant was besieged with calls offering everything from home sale assistance and financial counseling to outplacement services. After we had fielded these calls for some time, the decision was made to post such information on a plant bulletin board for employees, without any promotion or sanctioning from management. At the same time, company managers tried to outline the services the company would provide over the course of the closure so employees could discern what additional outside help they might need.

One of the services provided by the company was outplacement training. Since there had been fab closures at other company sites, the plant training council contacted the corporate employment group to help set up some outplacement training programs that had already been developed and used within the company. One of the newer human resource managers had come from a company that had recently shut down a plant. He had done business with a particular local outplacement consulting firm during that closure. Convinced that a professional outplacement service should conduct the training, he made efforts to influence the plant training council that this firm should train the employees how to write résumés, interview successfully, and build job search strategies. As it turned out, the in-house outplacement training was a three-hour program that would be compatible with plant operations, and the "professional" outside training was a two-day version that went into more detail than the council felt necessary.

When the training council decided against the outside program and in favor of the in-house one for reasons of costs, timing, and general appeal, the manager became intransigent. But the issue was finally resolved in the plant manager's office. The manager was reminded that the training council had the right and power to make whatever decision they felt was best. By that time, however, several members of the council sympathized with the human resource manager and agreed to try a one-day training program with the outplacement firm to test its merit. But only four people showed up for the session, and half of them left before the training was completed. The general reaction was that this outside training had gone into excruciating detail that few employees would need or want to use. When this was communicated to the manager, there were hard words exchanged between him and one of the council members. It was rumored that this manager, having previously worked with the outplacement service, had a vested interest in bringing business to the firm for possible future benefits for himself. After this point, the issue was dropped, and the training using the in-house version was conducted. The outside firm, however, was ultimately selected to run the company outplacement center slated to open in June.

Recruitment and Retention

The emotional reactions associated with the plant closure, coupled with the lack of a consistent company product direction, made it difficult for the company to recruit for other company sites from the pool of local technical employees and engineers. Many of the local plant engineers, particularly designers, strongly resented the company and the president for what they considered to be an irresponsible decision to close the plant. Many of the experienced design engineers, who happened to be in great demand in the industry, had chosen to work for the company despite its unprofitability and eroding prestige in the industry over the past few years. They were not about to be talked into relocating with the company elsewhere. Several designers attempted to negotiate a design center for the company in the Utah area. Many of the more talented and experienced designers considered this the only way they would entertain notions of staying with the company. When the company refused to consider this as a viable option, the central group of six designers decided to relocate together to a major competitor in Oregon. These designers, referred to as the Design Six, included some of the best design engineers in the company: Jason, Mike, George, Nelson, Ron, and Brett.

One key senior designer, Jim, was left with a great dilemma. Jim had been designated as the new design manager for the remaining group to transfer with the company. He was also being strongly recruited by the competitor company in Oregon and pressured to join with the other designers who were leaving. Having spent his entire career with the company, Jim felt great loyalty to the company and was still recovering from the shock of the closure announcement. Jim had planned to stay with the company and was living in a home that had been in his family for many years. The thought of having to leave Utah created such conflicting emotions that he postponed the decision for some time. Nevertheless, he was interested in making a transition from an individual contributor to a role with more mentoring, and for that reason, the new position intrigued him.

As Jim agonized over the decision, one of the senior computer-aided design engineering managers who had accepted an offer to stay with the company became outraged by "management stupidity," because not enough was being done to retain Jim, whom he considered essential to the new group that was relocating with the company. After a lot of soul searching and heart-to-heart talks with friends and family, Jim accepted the opportunity to stay with the company, to the great relief of all the engineers remaining with the company. Needless to say, his decision influenced others in the design group who were concerned with the company's viability and were trying to decide whether to relocate with the company.

Initially, the engineering center was to be relocated to the California headquarters. But few if any of the engineers would consider relocating to California and accept the associated drop in their standard of living. So the new division vice president made a difficult, but necessary, decision to change the location to New Mexico. It was apparent that the Utah engineers had a very good reputation within the industry; their combined experience levels made the plant a key target for recruiting activity from the competition. In the face of a potential exodus of key engineering resources, the New Mexico site was finally designated as the technical center. Incentive bonuses were approved to ease the housing differential that was becoming a tremendous recruiting obstacle. Within a week after this decision became public, about half of the engineering group accepted offers to stay with the company. For the remaining engineers, concern about company stability continued to be the remaining obstacle to relocation.

Taylor, the fab engineering manager, was fighting hard to keep his process engineers from jumping ship early. He was a member of the management team overseeing the fabrication operation of the plant, the area that had been most implicated in the "malaise" from the previous management. This team, working hard to rebuild morale, had implemented a new team-based approach called "asset management." This new structure would give greater autonomy and control to the lower levels of the organization. Having invested a lot of time and energy in selling this approach to his engineers, Taylor felt embittered about the situation in which he now found himself. Until that point, Taylor had managed to convince his core engineering experts to stay with the company and invest in this management experiment that would potentially pay great dividends in terms of experience in creating an environment of innovation and collaboration in a high-tech world. Several of Taylor's engineers had chosen to switch career paths and try out a management-supervisory role in the new structure. Because of the closure, many now felt panicky, betrayed by these decisions. Some blamed Taylor personally.

Taylor saw no escape from the despair and hopelessness he was feeling. After over fifteen years with the company, he was ready to abandon the plant at the earliest opportunity. He wanted to remove the tremendous burden of responsibility he felt toward his employees and avoid the task of trying to keep the key plant operation going until the end of the year.

## Implications

### Maintain Positive Communications

Employees typically become the most hostile in the first few weeks after a closure or downsizing announcement is made. It is natural for employees to see themselves in an adversarial relationship with the company. Even local management is not immune from feeling anger and going through denial, which are common at this stage of a closure. Most employees will want to work through these emotions and diffuse the associated negative energy. Communication continues to be a critical factor at this stage.

Rumor control is a serious issue in communications between employees and management during the early stages of downsizing.

Even small rumors can cause serious damage if left unaddressed. Consistency in communications can be difficult when outside sources misquote or misinterpret the information the company provides. We discovered that if the press were interested in a particular angle of the closure, they would seek out sources to confirm that angle. When employees are not given adequate information, they will tend to speculate, reducing the already strained trust between company and plant. It is imperative that companies inform employees of all relevant closure or downsizing issues and let them preview communiqués sent out in the community for public consumption. This will not guarantee that miscommunications will not occur, but it will minimize the need for speculation and present more coherent communications. Managers must confront rumors openly so that they don't become widespread. With frequent work team meetings, these issues can be discussed, and employees can reason through the hearsay instead of reacting to it. Affected employees should feel welcome to express their feelings and to discuss them with other employees; however, displacement of anger and hostility to other victims is not appropriate. Local managers who will also be layed off often become the victims of this displacement and can become overwhelmed in dealing with employees' emotions as well as their own. Rather than ascribing blame, employees need to seek understanding and clarity about the situation and its ramifications. Understanding that all those at a closing plant will be affected, whether or not they relocate with the company, is an important step toward reconciliation and maintaining a community atmosphere at the plant. This sense of community can become the single most effective force in surviving a plant closure or substantial reductions-in-force.

Managers must try to respond positively even in the face of hostile and emotional employee confrontation. By being more available to employees, managers can help clarify information, dispel rumors, and encourage open and honest communication. Although managers may also want to blame the company, they must be careful not to reinforce employees' negative feelings. Without participating in counterproductive venting, managers can form a bond with employees by explaining to them their own difficulty in working through these emotions. Managers should express confidence in employees' ability to cope and should provide encouragement for responsible behavior such as staying productive and finding other employment. For those employees who seem troubled and unable to rebound, managers or supervisors can provide early detection and intervention and persuade those employees to seek the help they may need.

*Initiate Outplacement Strategies*

Rather than waiting to see what outplacement training options are proposed by employees, plant management should take the initiative to devise a plan that includes the criteria of meeting employee needs while avoiding conflicts of interest that can become politically volatile. At this point, fear and anxiety from both employees and management at the affected plant may lead some to pursue special interests that may in the long run be a disservice both to plant employees and the company.

For policymakers, it is important to be prepared to offer meaningful productivity and retention incentives to reassure employees that they are, after all, the greatest asset to the company. Have a plan to retain key talent within the company. Be prepared to discuss this plan with those employees, and if possible, take their input into consideration. Employees' anger will become a real force to be reckoned with if these incentives are only token in nature and not substantive financial rewards. The company must also prepare to deal with some employee anger and hostility as it attempts to recruit key employees to relocate. Most of the employees at the Utah plant who were selected for relocation had no desire to leave the state and were resentful that the company forced them to confront this decision. By contacting key employees with attractive offers immediately after the downsizing announcement, thus reinforcing their value, companies may be able to obviate this anger, guaranteeing these employees a viable safety net should they desire to pursue other outside job possibilities.

This is a time when most employees will either feel that they have been dealt with fairly or will band together against the company in search of some other means of redress. There is a very tight margin of error during this time; stories of employee treatment will spread rapidly throughout the plant employee community. If there is deliberate and concerted recruitment effort to retain employee talent to the end, loyalty will finally win out, especially if an equitable severance package is offered. To assure retention of key employees, the personality and individual needs of each recruitment candidate must be taken into account. Quick and easy formulas for deriving retention incentives are often perceived as insulting and biased. As much as possible, make every attempt to tailor these special incentives to individuals.

Stage 2: Anger and Denial

| Employees | Management | Policymakers |
|---|---|---|
| —Try to diffuse emotions<br>—Talk with other employees<br>—Don't displace anger to other victims<br>—Seek understanding and clarity about downsizing ramifications | —Clarify information; respond to rumors<br>—Be more available; encourage frequent communication<br>—Provide early intervention for unusually troubled employees<br>—Don't engage in blaming company<br>—Express confidence in employees and provide encouragement | —Prepare key employee retention packages<br>—Consider productivity incentives |

# 5  March
## The Bargaining Begins

$B$y March, most of us were essentially resigned to the finality of the closure. We all shared a common bond in our immediate destiny. We tried to create meaningful options and solutions to the problems that confronted us. Removing the obstacles and uncertainty became primary motivators. We sought negotiated solutions to our individual circumstances: the community sought restitution to maintain a stable tax base; customers wanted assurances that their vendor sources would continue to provide an uninterrupted supply of good products; the company wanted reassurance from the parent company that its viability would continue; and the parent company wanted evidence that the imminent restructuring changes would leave it with a more viable and profitable set of assets. The question became how many of these various and sometimes competing interests would converge.

### Organizational Changes

After a senior managers' meeting held early in March, some significant organizational changes appeared imminent. The Dutch parent company, which wholly owned the company, intended to absorb the company completely—including the name Signetics—by the beginning of the following year. Apparently, their displeasure over the company's lack of financial performance had created a need to be more directly involved with the daily supervision of the company. The reasons cited for this reorganization were the financial record of the company, the low margin products, and a realignment with the parent company's strategic focus on consumer electronics. The current company organization structure consisted of two product divisions and various staff functions, such as finance, sales, quality and reliability, and human resources. The future structure would merge all units into a U.S.-based business group with marketing, development, and production (MDP) units for each product family. Many of the corporate staff functions would be phased out over the next few years, and the current company president would leave the company as of the beginning of 1993.

Not much else was discussed on long-term implications to the business; it was assumed that the California headquarters would eventually be relocated to New Mexico. In addition, it was announced that a group of organizational efficiency experts from the parent organization would spend time in California reviewing and determining which overhead support groups would be reduced or eliminated. After these announcements, rumors once again moved through the plant. Some employees speculated that the parent company had simply lost patience with the U.S. operations. Consequently, negotiations between corporate management and our Dutch owners that had been ongoing since November 1991 broke down and turned into unilateral edicts. Further probing revealed that some high-level meetings would be held in May 1992 to outline the new company organization and clear up much of the ambiguity surrounding it. The division vice president had since chosen to spend very little time in the plant and seemed aloof from local plant strife. Needless to say, hostility toward him by Utah employees was evident and continued to grow as it became more and more apparent that he had been brought in by the corporate staff to help with the plant closure.

## Consistent Communications

Community relations deteriorated a bit in the ensuing weeks. The local mayor went public in the press with a five-point plan to "help employees survive the shutdown of the plant." The text of one newspaper article specified that the first layoffs would take place 20 March, with the majority of layoffs scheduled for 3 October. This conflicted directly with what plant management had communicated to employees. Internal communications indicated that the first layoffs would likely not occur before May or June, and the bulk of the layoffs would occur when the fab area shut down in December.

Once again, the plant management team found itself having to explain to employees a major discrepancy in what they were hearing from plant management and what they were picking up from the local press. The plant manager immediately contacted the mayor's office to find out where the mayor had received information. The mayor was defensive. She had received the information from a letter the plant manager had sent to the state regarding the plant closure. Referring back to this letter, the plant manager observed that the information had been taken entirely out of context. The letter in reference was an official communication sent to the state to conform to the WARN Act of prior notification in the event of a plant closure. The letter indicated no layoffs "prior" to 20 March; and the majority of layoffs would occur "beginning" the first part of October.

When this was explained to the mayor, she said she would be happy to clarify this with employees who contacted her office. But no official press clarification ever followed. The plant manager, through his involvement with the local community economic development group where the mayor's office was represented, made efforts in subsequent meetings to prevent further miscommunications with the community. As a further measure to win back the confidence of employees, the official letter in question was posted on plant bulletin boards.

Because of the community SOS group efforts, many plant employees began to hope that the plant might be bought and their jobs retained. Some went so far as to make industry contacts with businesses that might be willing buyers. But the chances of this occurring were less than slim because of the nature of the industry and the locale. So the SOS group began to publish periodically a memo to all employees, keeping us posted on the process and problems associated with finding a willing business partner. In one of the March updates, the following disclaimer appeared: "This group of volunteers is working and will continue to work diligently to find a successor [business]. We will do all we can to find a solution to this problem; however, we feel it is imperative that the labor force not rely on SOS for future employment prospects."

Retraining Programs

In response to the considerable local press coverage, the vice president of human resources came to visit the plant. He had apparently been instructed by the company staff to see what he could do to help provide resources and funds for retraining assistance to the Utah employees. The plant had applied for federal trade assistance monies (to the initial resistance of corporate management), and the company staff now seemed eager to reestablish employee relations at the plant. Human resources quickly developed a plan to fund both a retraining program and a "career reimbursement" program, and the plant manager pitched both to corporate officials. The career reimbursement program was designed to provide more open-ended funding for special training programs not covered through the targeted retraining classes. On hearing a very general overview, the vice president of human resources pledged his support to help expedite funding for these programs. Not long after his visit, the announcement was made that company funding had been approved.

One particular course covered under the retraining program, intensive computer training, was especially troublesome to get established. One of the larger local employers in the area had a vested interest in this training, because it prepared applicants to become certified in it's own company software and technology. Employees were targeting this company as a preferred future employer and were lobbying hard to get into the training course. Several of the training council members met with representatives of this company to see if they would help subsidize the training as a bargaining chip to have a more experienced applicant pool. As it turned out, many plant employees had connections with former plant employees at this company and were trying to persuade them to influence that company's willingness to work with the training council.

After a visit with one of this company's human resource people, it became clear that the company had already been inundated with applicants and résumés with related training and experience. No quid pro quo from this company seemed likely. Unfortunately, the people who signed up for the class were on their own. The costs to run this training program with forty-five students would consume 25 percent of the entire retraining budget. Undaunted, employees signed up in droves for this training, knowing that they would have to pay a good share of the training costs themselves. More employees registered than could be reasonably accommodated. Our dilemma now was how to select forty-five attendees from the nearly seventy interested employees. Many perceived this training as their stepping stone to a new career in the state.

Several groups in the plant began lobbying hard to ensure that their employees would be given first consideration in the selection process. As one possible screening method, it was proposed that the plant staff rule on who could attend. Fortunately, economics prevailed. In fairness to the other employees who were not interested in this type of training and in maintaining a balance of cost per employee for the overall training, it was determined that it would cost each employee $1,000 to participate in the certification course. Even so, the company would still pay the major portion of the cost for this course. In short, employees were self-selected, on the basis of their true commitment to the career field, rather than on easy ways to get hired by a local netware company.

## Release Date Negotiations

Certain individuals, particularly those in high demand in the industry, had tried to negotiate their release dates in order to guarantee their completion bonus payoff before leaving for another job. Several design engineers who quickly received offers began the negotiations. In one case, Nelson wanted to know what the legal requirements of the WARN Act were, so that he could begin the process of getting his sixty-day notice. He drafted a contract, stating that he was asking for his notice now; he would complete a list of tasks if this notice were granted to him. Taking the human resources and legal departments by surprise, Nelson persuaded his manager to sign this document. On hearing about this, the group human resources manager was outraged.

Immediately, word spread to the rest of the design community that this tactic had attracted a lot of attention, and several designers drafted similar contracts. The Design Six had all received offers from the same company in Oregon to begin work approximately at the same time. Ron, one of the six, began to make threats that if his notice was not delivered *soon*, he would walk out on several key projects and sue the company for severance policy violation. Another one of the six, George, offered a more palatable bargain. George maintained his interest in staying with the company if certain conditions were granted. Because he was one of the more senior designers with several key patents, management made sincere efforts to meet some of these conditions so that George might be enticed to relocate with the company. When it became clear that these conditions could not be met, George was one of the first to be granted his sixty-day notice.

George was the type of employee that any company would love to have—self-effacing and loyal, yet clearly one of the most productive design engineers in the group. George's several patent awards for the company involved his work on metastability. He was also highly regarded by his coworkers. Emotional turmoil erupted in the design group because individual engineers were boasting about getting recruited and about the job offers received from other companies. But George retained his perspective. His family was interested in moving to New Mexico, where his wife would be closer to her family, but they also had close friends in Oregon. Having spent his entire design career with the company, George was intrigued by the notion of moving to a different organization with new challenges and opportunities. At the same time, he had strong ties both to the Design Six and to his coworkers, who had decided to transfer to New Mexico.

In his discussions with management, George was very open about his situation and his desires, trying to be both fair to himself and aware of the company's needs. Furthermore, George worked quietly to convince some of his more arrogant and hot-headed coworkers to be more reasonable in their demands from and approach to the company. When George learned that management had failed to grant his requests, he carried no grudge or ill-will. He completed his final work assignments with integrity and commitment.

After talking with George and Jim, Nelson, another Design Six member, apologized for his impetuous behavior in drawing up the contract. He asked to be granted his sixty-day notice at the company's earliest convenience. After plant management was advised by the legal department that this "contract" had been signed by the manager, Jim, and was therefore probably legal, Nelson was granted a sixty-day notice retroactive to the date indicated in the contract. Addressing more aggressive tactics firmly, management warned Ron that if he continued to pursue his disruptive behavior, he might be terminated without notice or bonus of any kind. The plant staff met to review the situation with these six designers. They expressed concern that other employees might start pursing a similar strategy if these six were granted their notices. It was also clear, however, that the tasks assigned to these engineers were quickly drawing to a close, and there was relatively little work left for them to do. After much deliberation, notices were granted to these engineers at the same time management issued a general announcement to all employees that sixty-day notices would henceforth be granted at the discretion of the respective departments, and these decisions would be based on individual circumstances and work assignments. In order to preempt similar negotiations with other employees, managers quickly provided estimates of respective notice periods to each employee.

Relocation Negotiations

Approximately fifty employees, mainly engineers, had accepted transfers to go to New Mexico. Relocation issues and questions were getting addressed by human resources management but to some degree it appeared to be an exercise in discovery. Current policy needed to be updated, revised, or enhanced in order to deal with this large, group-move situation.

A real domino effect occurred as more and more key plant employees made their transfer decisions public. A critical mass of engineers, aside from the designers, also decided to relocate. Housing prices between Utah and New Mexico prompted these employees to make proposals for additional financial support, which they felt they needed from the company to make the move. These financial proposals ranged from $1,200 to $100,000. When the amounts of all these proposals were tallied, it became clear that the company would need to provide additional help to relocate employees, while maintaining a reasonable relocation budget at the outset. Rather than determine how many of the proposals were legitimate, the company decided to offer two- to four-month bonuses to the relocating employees, based on critical skill. Once this relocation issue was resolved, others quickly surfaced.

Some employees with small families argued to be allowed to move themselves and pocket the difference in what they saved the company. Others with large families tried to negotiate for more money, to be used toward securing a mortgage in lieu of monies used for temporary living. All kinds of exotic and interesting proposals were advanced. A relocation council was created to try and address these issues and achieve some consistency in what the employees were told. It appeared that the New Mexico plant had different relocation policies than both Utah and California. Some employees, the first to pursue a particular issue, were told one thing and later informed that a different decision had been reached. Frustration mounted at all sites. Corporate employment representatives were routinely sent to Utah to begin meeting individually with employees to work out specific family relocation needs. A relocation newsletter was established, and "Good Move" seminars were offered to control the anxiety and general upheaval the transferees were experiencing.

As more and more recruiting from industry competitors occurred, it became evident that if the company wanted to retain the "best" employees, it would need to respond with relocation offers more expeditiously. Several key employees confided that they were "fed up" with the "semiconductor syndrome" of industry expansions and contractions and wanted to move to more stable career fields and industries. For an engineer, this could mean starting over in another technical discipline with a commensurate cut in pay. For the white-collar professional or manager, it could mean sacrificing responsibility and pay to stay in the local area or transferring out of the state. Company longevity and education level played a significant role in determining who was flexible and marketable enough to either start over in a new career or transfer their skill set to another environment.

The New Mexico plant was pressured to forecast its hiring needs for the remainder of 1992 and into 1993. Negotiations took place between the vice presidents over each of the two plants to coordinate their budgets and head-count planning; job positions in New Mexico needed to be identified and posted so the Utah plant employees could bid for them. Responding to the concerns from the fab area, a special plea from the local plant manager to the vice president responsible for the New Mexico plant resulted in these negotiations taking place. The employment group in Utah later received nearly thirty additional position postings from the New Mexico plant, which now included more than just engineering openings.

If corporate management had realized the significance of peer pressure at the Utah plant in determining who would relocate with the company, surely they would have taken more careful measures to listen and respond to the outspoken concerns of informal leaders. These individuals advanced several proposals to corporate management that involved negotiable demands to make relocation a more attractive option. Most of the employees involved felt, however, that their proposals were given short shrift, and this confirmed their unwillingness to relocate with the company. Although a good number of employees—close to one hundred—eventually decided to relocate to New Mexico with the company, many identified key employees were not among those who decided to go, partly because of the way in which they felt they had been treated.

## Customer Negotiations

As one might imagine, with an announcement of a major plant closing, customers suddenly take a strong interest in finding out the details of what will happen to their products and the implications of transferring products from one plant to another. This is particularly an issue in the manufacturing of integrated circuits. Such manufacturing processes require exhaustive requalifications when they are moved from one fabrication area to another; new process engineering obstacles often occur in the transfer. Several meetings were held between the marketing-sales organization and key customers to present the rationale and plan for managing such a transfer. The customers were reassured that in the end, the advantages outweighed the disadvantages.

The formal presentation contained the following justification:

There are several issues that were considered as part of the rationale behind the decision to close the bipolar fab facility in Utah. If one were to summarize them in one statement, it would be as follows: In evaluating the future technology and product direction of the combined [company] organizations, it was fairly easy to determine that a 26-year-old, bipolar fab was an asset that no longer fit into the overall technology plan. The facility is 26 years old and in many ways was technologically out of date. This makes sense when you consider the fact that many of the products which are manufactured there are 10 to 15 years old. Capacity utilization was another consideration. In 1991, the fab ran at 35% capacity. While [company] was able to size the labor resources accordingly, the fixed costs associated with operating the fab remained constant. Each year, as the capacity usage shrunk, the total cost per wafer increased. In future years, as the bipolar standard logic market continues to decline, the capacity utilization would have continued to decline, thus further driving up wafer costs. The advanced equipment in the New Mexico plant will contribute to quality improvements and will drive down product costs. This equipment provides better vacuum integrity, reduces the likelihood of electromigration and provides more temperature uniformity. The Class 10 fab environment characterized by a much lower contaminate particle level will greatly improve the yields and infant mortality rate.

Special arrangements were made with key customers to provide last-time purchases. Customer representatives were also sent to both plant sites so they could receive first-hand information and investigate the strategies being formulated for successfully transferring their products. It was evident that everything possible was being done by the company to address all the concerns raised by the customers and to negotiate any special arrangements necessary to convince them that their products would be delivered on time and up to quality standards.

## Implications

### Clarify the Options

Once employees come to the realization that they must begin taking action and making decisions about their future employment, some will attempt to bargain with the company. Most often these are individual negotiations, but they can involve groups of employees seeking common interests (such as the Design Six at the Utah plant). Before making proposals, employees should understand the options that are available to them and the company's position regarding those alternatives. By generating as many career options as possible both within and outside the company, employees will have a better chance to optimize their situations.

Most important, when advancing a proposal to the company, an employee needs to understand the company's viewpoint and how it might respond. With this perspective, the employee is more likely to negotiate in good faith to match his or her own interests with that of the company's. Employees at the Utah plant discovered these were the kinds of proposals that were more likely to get approval. Some employees were more outspoken about their training needs and interests and lobbied hard for certain types of retraining programs. The silent majority, however, didn't press their needs or take advantage of on-site retraining classes. We discovered an effective strategy was to offer a variety of retraining options and to include specific on-site and community training classes and reimbursement for identified career re-education programs. Through these options, we found most employees taking advantage of some form of company sponsored retraining.

At this stage, it is important to understand organizational boundaries. Company management may not always be clear about what those boundaries are at first. It is when those boundaries are tested or crossed that they become most visible. Once they are identified, employees can work with local management to provide appropriate input on employee concerns and problems. Training needs and career services are areas where employees should give input. Groups of employees with common needs will typically get attention before individuals needs are addressed. Employees should take the initiative to find others with similar needs when planning to negotiate with the company.

### Plan Release Dates

Release date circumstances is another matter. Since these dates are typically very individual in nature and relate to specific skills, the company may be less willing to bargain. Employees who have the foresight to find others at the plant with similar skills who are willing to stay longer may be able to negotiate their release date for an earlier period. Companies will be most concerned about being fair to all employees at the expense of the few with specialized needs. In order to preclude substantial individual release date negotiations, companies should make every effort to formulate shutdown plans with commensurate head-count requirements as early as possible following the announcement. Release dates can then be determined by area needs rather than whenever they can be negotiated. Employee relations will suffer serious damage if enterprising employees are allowed to initiate this process. This is not to say that individual negotiations may not be warranted in certain cases. These exceptions, however, should be few, based upon critical skills, and should mutually benefit both company and individual.

Managers can help represent their employees' needs and concerns to company policymakers. Since supervisors have more experience in understanding the company's perspective, they can help formulate and present proposals that will be more acceptable and take into account the needs of the business. At the same time, supervisors will better understand the employees' perceptions and can work to find common ground. In considering process and policy recommendations, it is important for managers to know which are the minority and majority opinions of employees. Again, those managers who have spent the time to seek out both perspectives will find the most acceptance in negotiating terms.

At this point in the downsizing process, it is important to give the plant some latitude to make proposals that will benefit plant employees. If general guidelines such as financial constraints and nonnegotiable policy parameters are provided in advance, most of these proposals will not be unreasonable. Making such proposals provides the employees at the plant a feeling of partnership. In allowing for some bargaining and negotiations on subjects where plant influence is asserted, plant employee relations can be improved. Companies might want to leave some room open in typically proscriptive relocation policies for negotiations with employees who are being recruited for relocation. This allows employees additional flexibility and gives them the feeling that they are truly valued. Topics for negotiation could include everything from tailored employee benefits to work schedules and outplacement support. If everything has already been predetermined by management, plant employees will feel even more disenfranchised. At this stage, the Utah plant was able to successfully negotiate area shutdown strategy, specific determination of individual release dates, specific retraining plans and topics, and application of transfer policies within areas and between company sites. The downsizing or closure plan should allow for employee input, while making clear which areas remain nonnegotiable. If plant employees can begin to feel empowered once more, they will tend to take more control of their circumstances.

Stage 3: Bargaining and Negotiations

| Employees | Management | Policymakers |
|---|---|---|
| —Understand available options both within company and outside<br>—Try to understand company viewpoint<br>—Explore career alternatives<br>—Test organizational boundaries<br>—Provide input to management on concerns and problems | —Represent employees' concerns<br>—Help formulate and present proposals to company<br>—Seek out majority and minority employee opinions on process and direction<br>—Understand employees' perceptions | —Allow some plant discretion in applying policy during downsizing or closure<br>—Consider plant proposals<br>—Be clear about nonnegotiables |

# 6 April

## The Distancing Among Us

There are times when employees reach a point where it is clear that their interests and those of the company's are diverging. Ordinarily when this happens, a confrontation takes place to either bring an employee back to a point of common interest with the company or to cause their paths to separate. By April the policies and procedures had already been redefined and implemented, so there was little or no remaining energy left to maintain a common bond between the individual's and the company's best interests. Many plant employees felt that they had been cut adrift and left to navigate on their own without intervention.

Somehow, whether intentional or not, a gulf had been created between the Utah plant and the rest of the company. This distancing was also evident between the employees who chose to transfer with the company and the short-termers who remained behind to seek other career options. A mutual crisis like a plant closure can forge strong alliances that can also cause friction with other groups in the company. What seemed most galling to us in the plant was the apparent lack of empathy the rest of the company showed for our situation. The business-as-usual manner displayed by the rest of the company implied that everyone in the plant had come to terms with the situation and was busily engaged in whatever career pursuits they had chosen.

Local management often bears the burden of dealing with the strained relationships that develop between plant employees and the rest of the company. Unfortunately, the problem didn't just exist between plant and corporate. The plant employee community now began to unravel as employees started turning inward, becoming more self-focused. Work group and interdepartment conflicts surfaced. Almost everyone had to fight the tendency to withdraw from fellow employees and forget the bonds that unite.

## Employee Alienation

When the time arrived for the company annual performance review and salary increase (or focal point) process, Jim, the new design manager in the engineering group, suddenly faced the unenviable task of determining how much of a salary increase to assign his entire group of design and layout engineers, based on their performance of the previous year. Jim had not conducted any of the performance reviews with these people who had recently been his peers and were now under his supervision. Understandably, he paled at the prospect of having to face each of his new subordinates with their respective increases. Searching for ways to reward the people who had chosen to stay with the company and move with his group to New Mexico, Jim decided to grant an increase only to those who were staying with the company or remaining until the area shut down. This quickly ruled out the Design Six and other engineers who had announced their intention to leave and go to work with Intel, Motorola, and other close competitors.

Learning this, Ron, one of the Design Six, exploded. He stormed out of the design area, searching for some coworker support in his righteous indignation. Claiming that he had earned his increase from last year's performance review and that the vice president had said that everyone would be eligible for the annual salary increase, he chased down a human resource representative. "Lies, lies and more lies!" he yelled at the startled manager. "When are they going to stop telling us one thing and doing another?!" The human resource manager struggling to understand the assault, queried, "What is the problem?" Ron, continuing his attack, responded, "I distinctly heard the vice president himself say that we would all be eligible for a focal point increase, so why am I not receiving one?" Still trying to understand the issue, the manager replied, "Everyone who was eligible for an increase didn't necessarily receive one, and you need to speak with your supervisor if you have a problem with that." Ron's anger escalated, and his face reddened: "I'm going to press this all the way. They can't get away with this!"

By this time, a small crowd had formed in the hallway where the heated discussion was taking place. Philip, a layout engineer who faced a similar situation and had been unable to negotiate a completion date to coincide with his new job at Intel, joined in: "I heard the same thing promised, and I was also told that we would be able to get quick release dates." By this time, the human resource manager, Larry, began to show real concern. "Each of you individually needs to pursue your personal circumstances with your managers. You need to understand the company's perspective on these issues as well. You are more than welcome to contact the vice president and discuss this with him." With that, Larry turned on his heel and walked away, visibly shaken by the confrontations.

It was generally perceived by others in the plant that the engineering organization always got away with anything it wanted. Word had already circulated that the Design Six had received their completion dates. One of the fab managers approached Larry shortly after hearing about the exchange in the hallway to find out if indeed Ron and Philip had managed to get their way. On learning the details of the situation, he observed, "Everyone in the plant is watching what goes on to see who gets what as we're all looking out for our own interests now."

One particular key engineer, Nelson, seemed to typify the distancing that was taking place between the company and individuals. A very creative and innovative engineer, Nelson was known for his tenacity and belief in himself and his work. He had several patents to his credit and was also well respected by the other engineers. Once the announcement was made, Nelson did everything he could to rally the group around the idea of staying together. Appealing to his peers, he urged them to recognize what a great team they had and that few places would offer the same camaraderie and atmosphere that they had established in the company. As time went on, however, Nelson began to lose confidence that the company was looking out for the best interests of the engineers. He quickly turned from company advocate to dissenter and was instrumental in influencing some of the other key engineers to leave the company. When confronted with this change in behavior, Nelson realized that he was reacting emotionally and not rationally. In all candor, he admitted that the offer he received from the other company wasn't as good as the one he had received to stay with the company. Acknowledging that he was becoming a disruptive force in the group, Nelson agreed to leave quietly without further intervention in the affairs of his associates.

Plant Controls

The plant staff met each week to discuss policy and procedures and review the status of the closure activities. This group consisted of the plant manager and the equivalent operations manager in each of the different areas of the plant. Normally, the results of these meetings had been viewed as positive, or at worst innocuous, by the rest of the employees in the day to day functioning of the plant.

Recently, however, the staff had decided that it was necessary for them to approve any communications sent out to the employees, in order to maintain visibility and control of plant activities. In real terms, this would preclude support organizations and operations from communicating necessary information in an expeditious manner prior to the plant staff's approval. Benefits information, training class schedules, and routine reporting requests would all would be regulated and slowed down as a result of this new requirement. The immediate reactions to this request by the plant staff were disbelief, anger, and frustration—particularly from the managers one level down from the plant staff. They viewed the request as an intrusion on their domain and an unnecessary step that not only added to the bureaucracy, but infringed on their autonomy and the empowerment supported by the plant culture. Some chose to follow the request begrudgingly; others simply ignored it. By and large, things remained as before, and the plant staff chose not to push the issue.

Plant Communications

On 21 April, the company president held another plant employee communication meeting, the first since the January meeting when the closure announcement was made. Some employees were anxious that more bad news would follow. New rumors circulated that an earlier closure date would be announced. The president started off the meeting by dispelling these rumors. He reassured his audience that he was simply complying with his promise of holding quarterly communication meetings at each site. He proceeded to review the financial performance of the company, stating that March had posted a profit of $137,000; both product divisions were now profitable.

He unveiled company restructuring plans, indicating that the company would be fully absorbed and integrated with the parent-owner company sometime later in the year. The company name would disappear, appearing only as a brand name for the integrated circuits produced. Corporate support groups would be reduced or eliminated by the end of 1993, leaving two business groups that would report directly to the CEO of the parent company. The New Mexico plant would become a "megafab" for the U.S. parent company operations, doing foundry work in addition to its regular production. Shutdown plans, including specific schedules, for the Utah plant were reviewed by area. Finally, the president proudly announced that the Utah plant had passed the examination and certification for ISO 9000, a prestigious quality designation by an international standards board.

Rather than receiving the applause he was expecting for this announcement, the president was visibly astonished by the laughter and derision with which the employees greeted this news. On the defensive, he reacted with the comment, "I'm sorry, but I fail to see the humor. You should all be proud of this certification, as you all had a part to play in it. This certification makes the Utah plant one of the few U.S. wafer fabs ever to have received this distinction." The auditorium began buzzing with whispered exchanges as we all reacted in surprise that the president was not acknowledging the irony of the situation. One employee shouted out, "If we are so good, then why are you shutting us down?" Cheers and laughter reverberated throughout the room. Regaining his composure, yet avoiding the issue, the president waited until the noise died down and then turned the time over to one of his administrative vice presidents to cover some benefits issues.

A question-and-answer period followed a status review of the SOS group's progress. The questions were relatively benign and scarce. Asked by one employee what his personal plans were, the president responded that he really didn't know. He indicated that he would continue as president through early 1993 then make some career decisions. By this point, it was clear to most of us in the audience that the special rapport this president had developed with us over the past few years of his tenure was fading. Before this time, we felt that the president had a real understanding and connection with us, earning both our trust and respect. What remained now was a deepening sense of alienation.

Just before closing the meeting, the plant manager stood up and made some final comments: "I know that we are all still dealing with the reality of the plant closure, but I for one want to feel that I did everything I could to close this place with class. The plant is not closing due to any lack of performance, and we need to continue that good performance and be professional to the end." As he turned to sit down, the auditorium resounded with the enthusiastic applause these words evoked. Finally, someone had articulated the emotions that were percolating in the audience. Realizing that he had just been bested, the president dismissed the meeting with the words, "What more can I say?"

As often happens in a shared emotional event, the news of the meeting traveled throughout the rest of the company. Shortly after this, on one of his routine visits to the plant, the group human resource manager disclosed his views on what he heard had happened in the meeting. The president, apparently seeking validation for his response to the employees in the Utah meeting, had spoken with the group human resource manager. Feeling honored that the president would seek his advice, the human resource manager reassured him that it was okay for executives to display anger and emotion: "Sometimes we just need to show the employees that we don't agree with them or their perspectives." This manager genuinely felt it fully appropriate for the president to have responded the way he did. There were no further attempts by either the president or any of his staff to understand or reconcile what took place in this ill-fated employee communication meeting in Utah. At first, this event was referred to sarcastically as another example of how out of touch management was with our situation. When brought up as a topic of conversation later, however, it was typically mentioned with a note of sadness and melancholy. How could someone who seemed so in tune with us suddenly become so callous and insensitive?

It appeared to the Utah employees that the company president was unwilling to acknowledge their predicament. Since he symbolized the company, many employees concluded that the business would be run as usual without much consideration given to the plant. If he had discussed his remarks with the plant manager before the communication meeting, it would have been clear to him how inappropriate this communication was.

## Employee Resiliency

Brenda, one of the assembly production managers, played a significant role in the assembly operation. She spearheaded efforts to keep employees upbeat and positive, despite a climate of impending alienation and despair. Brenda had worked her way up from assembly operator to manager over the twenty years she had been at the plant. During that time, she had developed a philosophy of optimism and a can-do spirit that was contagious to those around her.

Brenda had invested a lot of time training the teams in assembly on how to be proactive and deploy self-management tools in their work. Now she was determined to have the teams harness that same energy and commitment in coping with the outplacement planning process just as they would tackle any normal work-related obstacle. She helped to influence the assembly management team to allow the production teams the time and flexibility they needed to work through their concerns and anxieties associated with the closure. Although Brenda herself had no management experience outside the company and lacked a college degree, she faced her own reemployment situation with equanimity: "I just feel that if you do your best and are forthright with people, things just tend to work out."

## Implications

### Continue to Pay Attention

Everyone involved in a plant downsizing, including plant employees and those at company headquarters, should recognize the potential employee relations nightmare that results if affected employees start feeling neglected and alienated. As upper management's attention to the reductions-in-force begins to wane and interest turns to the pressing needs of keeping the rest of the business intact, the danger of not adequately attending to plant employees' concerns grows. If negotiations between displaced employees and company representatives turn sour, the climate will quickly degenerate to threats and confrontation. Therefore, it is critical that plant employees feel they have successfully acquired the terms of separation that will meet their basic needs and enable them to complete their tenure without bitterness and recrimination. This requires the company's close attention to the evolving plant climate and employee sentiments.

Managers can help alleviate much of the tension and distancing created during the downsizing by fostering a climate where employees can network with one another and identify common solutions to their resulting problems. Through staying in touch with plant employee needs and showing a human face, the company stays connected while continuing to manage the business necessities. Managers and supervisors can make personal appeals to particularly disruptive employees and provide them alternative perspectives. When employees begin to see how their behavior negatively affects others, usually they can be persuaded to either keep their emotions private or to function more positively by focusing on enabling activities.

### Designate a Corporate Liaison

Identifying a management liaison between the plant and corporate can be a valuable strategy, especially if the size of the company is such that other plant sites now command corporate management's focus. This liaison functions as a mediator between the plant employees' and the company's interests, ensuring that proper attention is provided throughout the downsizing or closure time frame. Further, this liaison can maintain ongoing contact with the plant and allow employees to deal with a friend. It is not unusual for employees affected by plant downsizing to select a corporate management scapegoat on whom to displace their anger and frustration. Rather than react defensively, company management should accept this as natural and try to find ways to generate good will toward plant employees. Having someone in corporate management stay in close contact with the plant, to both interpret and respond to the employee community's needs, can prevent further employee relations problems. To employees who will soon be displaced, seemingly small communication blunders can become metaphors for how the company deals with the employee community. Employees need to sense that the company is empathetic toward their misfortune.

*Resist Tightening Control*

Company policymakers should also try to resist imposing tighter controls on the plant, reacting to the apparent turmoil and fearing the resulting loss of productivity. As in the Utah plant case, even local management may try to tighten controls by adding unnecessary levels of approval. Employees will balk at the loss of freedom at a time when they see their autonomy as one of the only remaining features at work. At this point, local managers will find themselves with a lot of time, freed up from production pressures and planning. There is a tendency to want to use this time to formulate centralized policy to control all the variables that occur during plant downsizing. Although some centralized policies are necessary, managers should resist the urge to create tighter controls on operations within the plant. A more effective strategy is defining policy triage where major concerns and problems are addressed centrally and local area control is continued for the remainder.

Managers can help reduce the tension between company and plant by identifying company policies that are not adequate for plant needs. They can be instrumental in ensuring that appropriate attention is given to the plant without the need for closer scrutiny and tighter control. By maintaining the dialogue between employees and company headquarters, local managers can prevent disastrous employee relations mistakes and keep the company sensitized to issues and concerns. More important, these managers must avoid contributing to the tendencies toward withdrawal and alienation at this stage in the downsizing process.

*Avoid Counterproductive Venting*

It is difficult for employees to function unaffected by their own experiences in obtaining benefits from the company. Nevertheless, employees should resist counterproductive venting and try to continue matching their self-interests with those of the company's. At this stage, if an employee slips into despair and alienation, it will be difficult for him or her to find the energy to complete work tasks meaningfully and endure the remaining period of time at the plant. Employees should attempt to reconcile their differences with the company in order to properly focus on meeting their obligations to the company, to their families, and ultimately to their prospective employers.

### Avoid the Business-As-Usual Attitude

Finally, those at corporate who continue to deal with plant employees should avoid the business-as-usual attitude and communications that would display a lack of empathy so dreaded by displaced employees. There *should* be a change in the way the plant's employees are treated. Sensitivity can be demonstrated in policy matters, business calls, meetings, and correspondence. The company liaison can manage the protocol, keeping the company from committing employee relations faux pas.

Stage 4: Distancing and Alienation

| Employees | Management | Policymakers |
|---|---|---|
| —Resist tendency to withdraw<br>—Try to re-energize and find meaning through networks<br>—Avoid counterproductive venting<br>—Try to match interests of company and self interests | —Identify inadequacies in policy<br>—Avoid contributing to withdrawal and alienation<br>—Ensure appropriate attention from company<br>—Maintain dialogue with employees and corporate representatives | —Provide company liaison to plant<br>—Ensure frequent and ongoing contact with plant<br>—Resist tighter control<br>—Avoid business-as-usual attitude |

# 7 May: Resignation or Renewal—Is There a Choice?

Inertia is a difficult force to combat. How much easier it was for us to reminisce on what could have been. Over the years, many careers were invested with the company in both good times and bad. We had unfulfilled dreams that needed only time to manifest opportunities. Now confronting each of us was the reality of those shattered dreams and hopes, and the futility of pursuing them further with the company. Some employees were holding on to their jobs in a spirit of complete abandonment and resignation, only delaying the need to reconcile with whatever the future would hold for them. Others in the plant had taken the time to investigate opportunities both inside and outside the company to seek for new career options, or simply new job assignments that would provide the experience, growth, and immediate challenge and would lead down new employment avenues.

Paradoxically, short-term benefits existed for some employees who postponed the decisions involved in reemployment. For now, they could focus their immediate attention and energies on the job at hand. This held particularly true for the operators in the fab area who knew that they must eventually contend with their impending outplacement, but needed the peace of mind they got from delaying those decisions until December. In a sense, they were renewing themselves in spite of their apparent circumstances by allowing the healing nature of work and peer networks to reinforce their sense of common identity. Conversely, those employees who continuously strived to find other employment and jumped at the first sign of opportunity seemed to be the very ones who failed to move through the process of renewal and harbored very bitter feelings toward the company, management, and sometimes even coworkers.

First Exits

Exit interviews were held with the Design Six. Several of these designers were unable to sell their homes in Utah. Consequently, they
were going to Oregon without their families until their homes were
sold. Clearly, this was a difficult and sensitive issue for those affected. Several of the six designers expressed a firm desire never to
return again to the company despite their fortunes with Intel. Ron
was quite cavalier about his decision to leave the company and predicted that the remaining design group would be calling them to
make job inquiries within a matter of months. Reed, another of the
six, was much more ambivalent about his decision, feeling some un-
certainly about whether this was the best move for him. After he
talked with the other five designers, it became evident to him that
perhaps a type of group think was occurring, by which they had
managed to convince themselves that this was really what they each
wanted to do.

Those of the six who were the most outspoken and confident on
the surface nevertheless had some misgivings about leaving the company and how this would affect their family circumstances. The ones
most apprehensive about leaving were relying on the others to dispel
their fears. A frequent comment from the departing engineers was, "I
can't go wrong with the composition of talent and expertise that is
going to Intel." After they left, their regular phone calls back into the
remaining design group in Utah painted a very rosy picture of how
wonderful it was to work at Intel. Further probing from their former
associates, however, revealed a more realistic picture, including some
admissions that they were putting in a lot more hours at work now
than ever before.

As he left, George seemed to be more at peace with himself than
the other five engineers. He was much more philosophical about the
situation: "I hate having to leave the family behind for now, but the
kids can stay and finish school and my wife will get the house sold
for us. Although I have no regrets about leaving, I'm still aware of
what I may be giving up." George was under no illusions about the
tradeoffs he was making in going from a highly cohesive and creative design group with lots of freedom and autonomy to one at
Intel that was sure to be more focused, intense, and restrictive. As

he finished his exit process, George parted with these words: "I hope I haven't burned any bridges—you never know how things could turn out."

Job-hunting momentum at the plant had increased for the engineers as more and more of them left for jobs outside the state. Motorola had become the preferred place of hire for the process engineers. Taylor, who had not received an offer from the company to go to New Mexico or from Motorola, expressed his mounting anxiety and resignation: "As more of the engineers leave, we are becoming very short-handed here, and things are falling apart in the fab. I, for one, don't plan on sticking around until the end to get left being the scapegoat for all the problems that will happen. It's going to get crazy around here." He determined to be "out of here" by July, fearing that by then most of the valuable engineers would be gone. Peer pressure had become tremendous since his coworkers had started touting their offers from other companies, and some were receiving as many as four or five. Those who stayed found themselves continually justifying why they were still around, contending with the perception that they were not good enough to get other offers.

## Complacency and Resignation

Frequently in this process, we found ourselves seeking reassurance that we were not slipping into complacency and resignation by comparing notes with coworkers. A type of support network had formed for those who planned to stay throughout the plant closure period. The difficulty mounted as friends within the department or work area left for other jobs. One such employee, seeking reassurance, expressed the difficulty in watching others leave and not having a plan for reemployment after the closure: "It's getting hard to keep challenged and engaged in productive efforts when my good friends are leaving. I keep asking myself, why am I sticking around?"

The human resource department had been provided additional incentives to retain key employees throughout the closure. They would help outprocess people and administer all the employee relocation, outplacement, and training programs. Thus, most of the employees in the department had made a decision to stay through the end. One of these employees admitted the strain he was feeling, particularly on Fridays, when exit interviews were conducted for the week: "We are expected to be professional and help shore up the morale for the plant, but who is doing that for us?" Leslie, an administrative assistant in human resources, was more philosophical about her dilemma: "I worry a lot about not finding another job, and I'm going to continue looking around. In the meantime, I'm going to take advantage of the retraining classes so I can try out a different career path when I leave." Shirley's perspective had an edge of humor: "I'll be here to turn the lights out when they close the doors. Then maybe I will think about what to do next."

Since they were not directly affected by reduced production schedules, support groups seemed to be a little more insulated from the day-to-day realities of the closure. Among many the motto was "business as usual." Because no change in their operations was visible, it was easy for these employees to become complacent about their work and future plans. When asked about plans for the future, some responded with an evasive "who knows?" and quickly walked away to avoid further probing. One engineering support employee, Jesse, claimed he had practiced a response to give whenever someone posed the ubiquitous question. "I've got time to worry about that later since I'll be around here until the end," he retorted. He admitted that this response belied the anxiety and stress he was actually experiencing almost on a daily basis: "I wake up with the fear and worry every morning now. My daily challenge is how to find ways to alleviate the worry either through some diversion or by trying to find some way to make progress, however small, toward getting a career plan together." Jesse had also been with the company for many years and was anticipating a sizable incentive bonus at the end of his completion date in December.

Not even employees planning to transfer with the company were immune from despair and resignation. Here again, company seniority seemed to play a significant role in the employee's perception of the degree of choice they faced. Alex, a highly valued engineer, expressed his general disappointment and disillusionment with the direction of the company. Since he had chosen to transfer to the New Mexico site, Alex was trying to justify his decision to some of the other undecided engineers. Always seen as an informal group leader,

Alex realized he had some influence over his colleagues and wondered how he could be a positive force to them when he couldn't yet find good evidence to feel comfortable with his own decision. Without benefit of a specific company product plan and customer base, Alex was finding it difficult to point to any tangible success or solid company progress that he could use to bolster the growing pessimism and skepticism over the company's future stability. Alex and others in his group ascribed culpability to the new division vice president, who had yet to deliver on his promise of a revitalized product division, and their animosity grew.

Many employees at the plant were looking for confirmation of the feelings they were experiencing at this stage of the closure. Work groups wielded tremendous influence in the attitudes of employees. Those group opinion leaders who were negative and harbored ill will toward the company and their circumstances tended to foster resignation and hopelessness in others. The most productive groups were those whose informal leaders had found meaningful ways to cope and were positive and upbeat about the future. These were the same groups that were the most productive both at work and in their reemployment searches.

### Government Funding

We received word that the U.S. Department of Labor had rejected the company's request for trade assistance funding for employees who wished to return to school or needed to relocate from the state as a result of the closure. The company had been approved in previous years under this same Trade Readjustment Assistance (TRA) Act due to the downsizing and laying off of employees that resulted from foreign competition. So, the news came as quite a shock, particularly to the operators who had most heavily counted on receiving this funding support. Employee communication meetings were held on each shift to deliver the news and report on the status of the company's financial performance to date.

General dismay was apparent in the faces of employees in the communication meeting. It didn't help that the plant manager reported a loss for the company year-to-date of almost $2 million. Despite the disappointing news on the federal funding status, the company announced that it would now seek state funding. It would also make an appeal to the U. S. Department of Labor to reevaluate the company's eligibility for federal funding. Nonetheless, for those who were attempting to make future plans involving schooling and who needed confirmation on funding, the news was disheartening. The questions that followed the presentation centered on the appeal process: How long would it take? What was the company doing to provide additional documentation? Who could the employees write to in Congress to help make the case for the company? The security of generous incentives to return to school when they left in December now eluded many of the fab operators.

After receiving word that the federal funding would not be available, the plant manager and SOS committee lobbied hard with the state to provide some help. With support from the governor's office, state monies were pledged in the event that the appeal was denied.

## Organizational Changes

Expectations in the engineering organization were dashed when it was announced that the head of the parent company's integrated circuit division in Europe would retire at the end of the year. In addition, the company's president was leaving around the same time. These events virtually assured employees that there would be little or no change in strategic direction, as was hoped. Corporate staff had just participated in high-level meetings in Europe, with the ominous moniker "Centurion II." The official word from these meetings was that a few organizational changes would occur, and these would align the company more closely with the business structure of the parent company. Any strategic changes, however, would be postponed into 1993. This triggered more key employee resignations and did nothing to change the laissez-faire climate in the plant.

## Employee Surveys

An employee survey was conducted in the plant to obtain feedback on how employees were faring with the closure and to gather specific information on the effectiveness and rate of use of the outplacement and retraining services offered by the company. For the most part, employees were fairly positive about the specific training and out-placement programs they had taken part in. Most planned to partici-pate in one of these programs. The programs were mostly rated good to excellent, with a few ratings of fair to poor. More revealing, how-ever, were the written comments of employees. Again, most were positive and reflected a sense of renewal as employees appeared to be coming to terms with their job situations and taking advantage of the retraining and outplacement services. Samples of these comments follow:

> I am relocating to New Mexico with the company and would have liked a little more time to check out other market sectors before having to accept a relocation offer. But I understand the company's position too.

> I am actively pursuing bids that I'm qualified for in New Mexico. In the meantime, the company-sponsored retraining program efforts are excellent!

> I am very grateful that we have as much time as we do! It's nice to be able to think and plan our future as compared to giving us no-tice Friday that the plant would be closed Monday. I think that [the company] has been very good at helping us and trying to make the best of a bad situation.

> I feel [the company] has tried to do all they can to help us find other employment with their outplacement services and also with education. Thank you.

Some of the comments from the survey suggested that a few em-ployees still felt very bitter toward the company. Those employees harbored ill-feelings that carried over into whatever efforts the com-pany was making in their behalf. For a few of these employees, noth-ing would compensate for the blow of being forced out of a job. Here are a few of these employees' comments:

I'll *never* work for another European-owned and managed company again. I'd rather work for a Japanese firm. The Japanese at least know how to make money and how to reward hard work and loyalty!

[Some of] these courses are, for example, eight or ten weeks long and are costing a substantial amount of money to the employee. The reimbursement allocation is only $200 per quarter. It wasn't our decision to have to find new employment at this point. I have over ten years of employment with this company. Now I have to go to school to be retrained at another type of job. Just because I don't have two years to take out of my life to go to an accredited college, so as to be reimbursed for this cost over time, doesn't mean I shouldn't be reimbursed for what I have put out for the [training] course already.

You are not doing anything for people staying [transferring] with the company, and everyone else's interests are not company-oriented. The transferees are not supported well enough because people are more interested in studying for their new careers. . . .

The shock around the Utah closure comes directly from [our] knowledge of the product-base running in the fab and the comparative wafer costs which clearly make the Utah plant closure a financial disaster for the long-term prospects of the company.

Other comments that conveyed a continuing sense of resignation and despair included a wish that the company would apply pressure to the local community college to get employees into certain programs that accepted only a limited number of students each year. Some found fault in the perceived lack of flexibility in the scheduling of courses, which didn't accommodate their personal needs or schedules. Evidently, there were employees who felt that the company owed them for taking away their jobs. Some wanted the company to take full responsibility for placing them in new jobs.

Finally, it was interesting to note the range of descriptions of the employees' reactions to the closure announcement in January. Whereas most expressed shock and surprise over the news of the closure, a large number claimed they "saw it coming." The great majority of responses indicated that the one positive aspect of the closure was the amount of time given them to prepare for their own departures from the company.

### Employee Relations Initiatives

We had reached a point when the gnashing of teeth over the closure had gone beyond the tolerance level, both for the company and most of the employees. Those that continued to moan and complain about their circumstances were finding fewer and fewer sympathetic ears willing to listen to their remonstrations. Since most were moving ahead with plans for the future, there was among the employees an increasingly forward-looking attitude. The company was working on a program to provide transition and adjustment training to the employees to promote their sense of empowerment and enable those who were still struggling to cope. In addition to this training (also offered to spouses and children), there was a concerted effort to secure funding from the state for postemployment education benefits. Still recovering from the blow of being denied federal trade assistance funding, plant management was applying pressure to the state to deliver on its promise to help the employees through the Dislocated Workers Assistance program.

As a gesture to show his support to the get-on-with-it climate, one employee typed up and posted a note:

> We have suffered from bad management. We were encouraged to [work] for other fabs, which inevitably led to the closing of the Utah fab. I am angry that my longest and dearest friends will no longer be my associates. But [parent company] is currently laying out a lot of money to move us to a modern fab and to get us to design parts that can be sold. We are being well paid to do interesting work. We need to stop mourning and start working hard.

Next to this employee's office was a cryptic sign with the word that further reinforced his message: "QWITCHERBELIAKIN" (quit your belly-aching). Because he was a well-respected senior employee,

the communication had a positive impact in the work area and resulted in less counterproductive behavior.

Rather than resigning himself to the fact that the only viable option at the moment was to transfer with the company to New Mexico,
one employee decided to hedge his bets. He accepted the offer to
transfer and negotiated a later transfer date with his manager, who
was also transferring there. This would allow him to keep his family
in Utah, travel back and forth from New Mexico, and still take advantage of the flexible relocation benefits. Since his transfer date was not
until the end of the year, he could further investigate the area, job,
and company stability and still keep his options open should a better
job opportunity surface in Utah. Because this employee was a key
individual in the group that was transferring, the decision was easier
for his manager, who was going out on a limb to grant this exception.

Up to this point, there had been very little turnover of employees
leaving for other work. The plant head count was still more than 900
employees, and an average of six to seven were leaving each month.
May was when some of the release dates for scattered positions
across the plant occurred. Most of the release dates were to begin in
July, with the bulk of the engineering group going in August and the
remainder of the plant operations dates occurring in December. Individuals were carefully considering before leaving and giving up a lucrative retention bonus to stay until their completion dates.

## Implications

### Encourage Supportive Activity

Eventually, most employees at the affected plant will weary of the
negative energy surrounding the downsizing, and they will attempt
to find ways to build a more productive climate at the plant. As this
occurs, a renewal process can take place within the employee community, built on mutual encouragement and support. Unfortunately,
companies may have little sway in how group attitudes form. By being sensitive to this employee group dynamic, however, managers
can attempt to minimize the negative effects of company bashing and
resignation by exposing these employees to others that are engaged
in constructive renewal strategies. This process cannot be contrived
artificially, nor can it be manipulated by management. Once it does

occur, however, it can be encouraged and nurtured, primarily through communication and cross-fertilization. If provided an opportunity, employees can become the most effective employee relations cheerleaders.

The renewal process comes sooner for some than others, and there are those who never quite experience it. Those individuals who become proactive and make choices about their careers can help others through renewal. An employee bulletin board can serve as a means for employees to share their job search experiences and contacts. Team meetings can be structured in such a way to provide networking or sharing time to discuss ideas for renewal, including tips on re-employment strategies. In some cases, work groups can practice interviewing and job-seeking skills collectively as they search for re-employment and go together to apply for positions. The sense of community among employees is enhanced through these experiences and will tend to remain productive as energy is rechanneled.

Employees who are effectively finding ways to adjust their careers and move forward can become important examples to others. As they hear about how coworkers have adjusted to and perhaps even benefited by their experience, employees find strength in each other's successes. It is mutually reinforcing for employees to help one another and provide the support they need to endure this period. This is not to say that management should rely solely on employee support to meet employees' needs, but should certainly acknowledge and facilitate this process. Coupled with the aid the company must provide to all displaced workers, employee support networks can become one of the most powerful forces to propel the critical mass of employees into self-renewal and revitalization.

### Seek Funding

Funding is obviously a critical issue in generating options for employees. Companies must explore all available funding including government and state grants. Someone should be assigned to investigate these sources of potential revenue which can have a tremendous impact on employee renewal and retraining. Companies that have taken the time to develop such community networks will have more funding support possibilities. Research into these funding sources is a critical step in any plant downsizing. As we discovered at the Utah plant, training assistance grants (TRA) can help facilitate the out-placement process and enable employees to make the necessary read-justments. Managers should be aware of the outplacement needs of their employees in order to pinpoint areas of greatest potential bene-fit. Even if these funding sources are not initially granted, as we dis-covered later, sometimes tenacity and additional data can pay off.

### Use Employee Surveys

Employee surveys can provide a useful means of identifying em-ployees' needs during the downsizing process. Although they can also function as a source of venting, they should not be conducted solely for this purpose. The reasons for such surveys should be clear at the outset—and expressly for benefiting employees in some tang-ible way. The Utah plant received a number of requests to conduct research surveys to collect data on plant closures. This kind of survey should only be offered on a voluntary basis and should not be spon-sored by the company. Employees tend to resent being subjects in such studies, especially if the surveys serve to remind them of their vulnerability. Employee surveys are a good ongoing source of infor-mation to keep management in touch with employee concerns and desires. By the same token, companies should be realistic and forth-right about what can and cannot be funded. Raising then dashing employee expectations can be one of the most devastating elements in an already difficult climate.

### Conduct Exit Interviews

When the first batch of release dates triggering employee exits oc-cur, many eyes will be on the plant to see how these employees are treated; coworkers will be attentive observing the process to find out what is in store for them, other groups in the plant will want to know about any special allowances given to these employees that might affect them, and often the local press will be close by to interview departing employees and capture their viewpoints about the reduc-tions-in-force.

Although this process is difficult for both company and em-ployees, it is important that time is taken to provide proper exit inter-views and allow departing employees the chance to discuss their feel-ings about leaving. In some cases, key employees who have been offered jobs with the company may be having second thoughts about leaving and wish to reconsider or simply be assured that they can return if their new job prospects don't work out. More important, if handled sensitively, this process can provide employees with a sense of reconciliation, a sense that their final interaction with the company was both compassionate and positive.

Stage 6: Regeneration and Renewal

| Employees | Management | Policymakers |
|---|---|---|
| —Engage in contingency planning—exercise creative options<br>—Look for success patterns and learn from other employees' experiences<br>—Establish networks and contacts both inside and outside plant | —Help facilitate networking and cross-fertilization<br>—Allow job searching on company time<br>—Share personal strategies with employees<br>—Celebrate employee successes<br>—Develop an effective exiting process | —Help to forge community contacts and alliances<br>—Pursue all available funding sources<br>—Collect employee need information |

# 8 June
# Rebuilding Our Future

There came a time during the plant closure process when a new organizational reality finally settled in and a type of reconciliation took place for the affected employees. Evidently this was a much longer process for some than others, and those who failed to come to terms with it often abruptly left the organization. Our values and beliefs regarding organizations rose to the surface, and suddenly we reached a new level of awareness about ourselves. One impulse was to try to make sense of this new organizational reality in order to resolve, for ourselves, the benefits of remaining in the organization for its duration. By the same token, many realized the often unhealthy dependencies we had come to take for granted in our relationship with the organization.

Misplaced loyalty was perhaps the most common dependency for those who had remained with the company their entire careers. One twenty-five year company veteran bemoaned the trust he had placed in the company in assuming that if he continued putting in ten hour days often six days a week, he would have a job for as long as he wished to stay. Realizing the tradeoffs he had made in his personal life, this employee resolved to become more balanced and put in his remaining time with the company in forty-hour-a-week increments.

Renegotiating and reconciling a new relationship with the organization became a liberating process for some of the employees. Now, suddenly they could become free agents who really answered only to their own conscience and sense of principles regarding the time they put in and the nature of the work they contributed to the company in the remaining time. A novel construct arose, creating for some a new synthesis of individual and organization in which choice became the byword. At best, they could now become masters of their own souls and destiny. At worst, they faced a pattern of work behaviors and ethics that would no longer be supported.

## Patterns of Work Ethics

Now that we were nearing the halfway mark on the way to the closure, interesting behavior patterns surfaced. Many of the employees who engaged in questionable work conduct no longer seemed to feel a need to hide their values or behavior for fear of reprisals from the company. Once-surreptitious actions now were out in the open. For instance, it was not unusual to see people skip out early on Fridays. Whereas in the past, this might have been the case for a few employees on Friday afternoons, it appeared now to be the norm—and not just for an afternoon. In some cases, attendance practices had eroded to the extent that entire areas appeared shut down on a given day. Managers could be as bad if not worse than their employees. If there was any confrontation, it was typically by a fed-up coworker who broached the issue.

One such occasion arose concerning the employment status of a married couple who worked in the engineering area. Both had accepted offers to work elsewhere and had been trying to negotiate for an earlier release date than the one granted. On the week they were to exit and receive their completion bonuses, a coworker spoke to someone in accounting, alerting that person that the couple had already started work with the other company. This led to an investigation with human resources on the appropriateness of paying them out a completion bonus and on regarding how their time off was being accounted for. The manager of this couple was brought in to the plant manager's office and questioned on what arrangements had been made to allow this couple to start work elsewhere before having officially left the company and to still receive compensation. When it became apparent that details such as how they were charging their time had not been properly attended to, a plan was quickly formulated to allow nothing improper. Time cards were forwarded to the couple at their new company, instructing them to use their remaining vacation and unpaid time up to their last official date at the plant. Nonetheless, news of this episode traveled throughout the plant via the employee network and led to a more vigilant practice of accounting for people's whereabouts.

In the fab area, a case of an operator misprocessing $300,000 worth of wafer lots raised the issue of sloppy workmanship and the lack of attention and care by some employees. All eyes were on the fab managers to see what they would do for follow-up to this incident, since the dollar value of the error had received companywide attention. Initially, one of the fab managers accused several of the fab supervisors of not following through with the requisite documentation and disciplinary actions expected whenever such an episode occurred. On further investigation, it appeared to management that there was a real variance in how wafer losses were handled among supervisors and the expectations of these supervisors concerning such errors. A comment by Taylor implied that fab management itself had lost control of the fab environment and employees' work habits: "I still want to be out of here by the end of the summer. It's getting just too difficult. We're losing control fast."

Regrouping to try and mitigate the rapidly disintegrating climate, Taylor, the other fab managers, and the plant manager discussed the need to orchestrate some sort of values confrontation with the fab supervisors. They felt strongly that unless some drastic course correction occurred, performance would continue to erode as the closure drew nearer. A meeting with all the fab supervisors to deal with these issues was planned for the following week. Meanwhile, word leaked to the operators that a powwow of major proportions was being scheduled, triggering fear of a backlash. In the monthly plant employee communication meeting held by the plant manager, this was the first topic brought up during the question and answer period. One fab operator on swing-shift stood up and asked what was going to be done now to the operators as a result of the large dollar loss incurred. He gave a short speech about the fear of reprisals from management that all the operators in the fab shared, along with the concern that there would be a reversion to the autocratic style of management they had experienced in 1990. They still had vivid memories about the overtime directives fab employees had received in the summer of 1990 when the push from corporate for more production was met with demands by management that operators put in "excessive" daily and weekly overtime hours. When they had protested to their supervisors, the operators sensed that these managers were unwilling or unable to represent their concerns, citing their own fears that they would be subject to dismissal for not following through on these overtime demands.

A round of applause followed, signaling general agreement from the audience. Attempting to add some perspective to the issue, the plant manager, Brent, responded with his own short speech on the need for discipline and collaboration. He acknowledged the concern of the fab operators by assuring them that there would be no return to the old style of management, nor a general crackdown. Brent also asked operators to work with their supervisors and attempt to become part of the solution to this general lack of discipline. Extending a challenge to all, he exhorted the audience to continue to do their best, taking pride and ownership in all of their work.

Not all were convinced by his message, and some skepticism still showed on the faces of the operators leaving the meeting. Later in a discussion with the fab managers, Brent advised them to proceed with caution in their meeting with the supervisors scheduled for the following week.

While this controversy continued, the fab supervisors had been watching closely and discussing it among themselves. Their perspective on the problem was considerably different from that of the operators or the managers. Many of them had been with the fab for eight years or more and had witnessed different management regimes and philosophies, including the current "asset management" philosophy. Since the fab had been divided into five different asset groups with a manager over each, there had been problems with consistency. Each group wanted to create it's own methods of operation. Supervisors found this disconcerting at times and had tried to raise the issue before. Not wanting to make waves, most of them simply went along with their asset manager's direction. As three of the five asset managers left, the remaining two managers consolidated the fab structure underneath them. Now suddenly, these two remaining asset managers faced the daunting task of confronting the different methods and practices being followed by their supervisors.

As thirty fab supervisors filed into the room where the meeting would be held, each seemed to register the range of emotions on the issues to be discussed. Everything from eagerness to guilt and reluctance to anger showed on their faces. One of the asset managers,

Karen, began by reviewing the expectations regarding fab disciplines and housekeeping procedures. After sensing the need to get feedback from the group, she turned to the group of supervisors to ask for ideas on how to implement these expectations across the board. Some of the supervisors immediately volunteered their input, which was captured on chart paper. About half were willing to participate and provide some ideas and comments. The rest of the group sat quietly, trying hard not to display their reactions to what was being said. In the responses given, there was clearly a diversity of opinion on what needed to be done and to what degree the problem of inconsistency existed in the fab. One supervisor, who seemed to strike a chord with several of the others, expressed concern over what he perceived to be the prevalent attitude of the operators. "If I attempt to go into the fab and ask the operators to do more than they are doing now, I will hear, 'What are you going to do to me if I don't? I've already been fired.'"

At this point in the meeting, Dan, one of the supervisors who had been very quiet, spoke up: "Let's focus on the individuals who have problems and try not to group-think this issue by doing what we have always done. We have to be realistic and pay attention to the feelings we all share over the plant closure. If you are telling us to dump our Save A Wafer program and go back to the traditional disciplinary action procedures, I can support that. I just need to know what you want us to do."

Save A Wafer was a program established in one particular asset section in the fab. If an operator made a mistake and scraped any wafers, rather than management subjecting the operator to disciplinary actions, a team composed of the supervisor and operators would meet and discuss what had happened and take corrective actions to ensure that the problem didn't recur. This program had generated great resentment from operators in other asset sections who were not participating and consequently were subject to the normal disciplinary procedures when they caused scraps.

Dan's comments triggered reactions from most of those supervisors who had remained quiet up to this point. Suddenly the room was buzzing with supervisor responses to what had just been said. Several took issue with Dan; others simply wanted to interject another viewpoint. Finally, the other asset manager, Leonard, intervened. He thanked the supervisors for all their input. "We all have a role to play in ensuring that the fab is managed fairy and consistently. We need to help people come to terms with the plant closure and by the same token appeal to their sense of pride in their work. We would like each of you to prepare a plan to review with both Karen and me on what you will do to deal with the problem we have presented and improve our overall effectiveness on the floor." On that note, the meeting adjourned.

Later, both asset managers reviewed the meeting in light of some additional feedback given by some of the attending supervisors. Whereas most supervisors had responded favorably to the request for support of the expectations and were discussing this subject with their people, a few of the supervisors felt differently. Apparently, some were offended by the "lecture" they had received in the meeting. They felt they were already doing everything they had been asked to do. If anything, they believed the problem to be with management. Rather than turn defensive to this feedback, the asset managers decided it was best to continue with individual follow-up with each supervisor to determine what each of them was doing with his or her operators. In addition, the fab management team decided to comply with the request by Brent that he monitor the morale of the fab through employee luncheons held each month. These luncheons would involve the supervisors as well. The general conclusion from this experience was that it was best to follow a more low-key approach to future problem resolution, both to avoid offending the sensibilities of operators and supervisors and to promote the idea that we were all in this together.

As all supervisors in the fab hunkered down to comply with the newly defined procedures on housekeeping and wafer scraps with their operators, all eyes fixed on the fab. Much was at stake in keeping the employee morale high through this period. If the operators felt they were being treated too harshly, the fab could lose the good will between the operators and management, and the operators could quit. Since everyone in the community knew of the impending closure, it was becoming very difficult to replace people when they left. Furthermore, the fab could not afford to free up any resources to train new temporary employees. The remaining operators in the fab area were the most senior and experienced. Corporate management was also relying on production of good wafers to continue to retain customers who were already leery about the transfer of products from the Utah plant to New Mexico. As it turned out, prudence pre-vailed among both the supervisors and operators on the issue. More disciplinary actions were taken, but only in cases in which they were unequivocally warranted. The crackdown feared by the operators never really materialized.

## Outplacement Center

To help employees with the process of rebuilding their careers, the company opened an on-site outplacement center euphemistically called the Career Transition Center. In the first week of operation, close to four hundred employees (almost half) visited the center ei-ther out of curiosity or because of actual interest in using the facility. Some of the services offered to employees in the center included indi-vidual counseling sessions with job placement counselors, job post-ings both for local and out of state positions, résumé consulting and support, career guidance tips, workshops on starting a business, out-placement training (including telephone skills, job-hunting tips, and interviewing). Since it was already determined that a designated con-sulting firm would staff and run the center, the plan and costs for the center had already been approved through the necessary levels by the human resource manager.

Whether or not it proved to be a success, the center was providing the company an employee relations gold mine both inside the plant and within the community. Just by having the center available, em-ployees were leaving with the attitude that the company was doing all it could to speed their reentry into the job market. Early reports from employees indicated that the center didn't have up-to-date post-ings; most were from outside the local vicinity. As it turned out, the firm managing the center had brought most of the early job postings with it from other sites it had been servicing. Despite this initial con-cern, the feedback from the employees using the center continued to be mainly positive.

## Organizational Changes

News from a visiting corporate manager indicated that the parent company organizational changes, which were anticipated to have occurred during May, were now imminent. The long-awaited and arguably needed restructuring, affecting both the company and affiliate plants, was to be announced in a few weeks. Intimating that the changes would be broad-based and significant, the manager offered his views on how this would affect the company. Having spoken to the company president, this manager admitted that the president realized he had made a mistake in prematurely announcing his early departure in 1993. As is natural when these announcements are made, people assumed that the incumbent was a lame duck and would no longer be interested or involved at the same level as before.

In this case, the president himself became somewhat disengaged in company decisions and strategies. This disengagement began to snowball as soon as the president announced his departure. Apparently, he was just becoming aware of this problem and was now in the process of attempting to become involved again in the larger scheme of company dealings. This president had never been in a position with a company in which his competence had been so significantly challenged and the business results so disheartening. Perhaps he had finally come to terms with his failings in the company and had decided that he was not quite ready to leave without an eleventh-hour effort to make some positive impact. Most of us in the plant viewed his reinvolvement favorably, since despite our recent differences with his views, we had been saddened by the withdrawal of this once very popular company figure.

## Recognition and Empowerment

A plant recognition committee had been formed and chartered with the responsibility to seek out methods and activities to boost morale for the remainder of the year. Each operational area had traditionally approached recognition somewhat differently over the years. Rather than stage plant recognition events as a whole, the plant committee decided to coordinate their activities and budget to be somewhat consistent, while still maintaining their separate group identities. The administrative support group decided to stage a luncheon each month that would include contests, drawings, and giveaways. Deciding what to celebrate became a little more difficult than determining how to do it. After some deliberation, the theme was to be the survival of all those remaining employees who were keeping the plant going to the end. Each month to announce the event, a flyer was sent to all administrative support employees, with a candy bar attached to attract interest and prevent the flyer from getting a pre-emptory toss in the garbage can.

In addition to these separate events, the plant committee recognized the need for a few plantwide activities. A traditional plant amusement park day was designated, with associated contests. There was also some discussion of a plant reunion toward the end of the year for all former company employees. These events seemed to help some of the employees get through the summer months as they watched their coworkers starting to leave the plant for other jobs.

The assembly area had realized some gains in allowing teams the time and participation in planning the remaining assembly production schedules. Brenda felt strongly that as a result, the employees would be more committed and supportive in maintaining the quality and productivity levels needed to finish off the work. She spent much of her time running interference for her employees, advocating their needs and interests to the plant staff. She was someone whom most of the assembly employees trusted to speak for them, and she was typically successful in getting management to address their interests.

Believing firmly that the needs of the area had to come first, Brenda had not as yet taken the time to generate a résumé. She was one of the few managers in the plant who had hardly missed a beat in adjusting to the closure process, and she acted as she would have if it had just been another typical assembly schedule adjustment. Brent was impressed with her efforts to keep the assembly area productive and found little cause to question or deny her requests for plant management support. Brenda had become a beacon of light to many in the plant, who saw her as a refreshing change from the absorbed self-interest of some of the other managers.

## Company Donations

The company donated $10,000 to the SOS committee to aid in its efforts to find a buyer for the facility. Intended as a gesture of good will and support to keep the activities of the committee alive, the donation received considerable attention, both from the local press and from plant employees. Some of the employees wondered about the propriety of such monies changing hands with local government, perceiving it to be a way for the company to clear its conscience over the closure. Others were even more cynical, viewing the donation as a sort of company payoff with strings attached to ensure that the plant would receive cooperation from the community in achieving a smoother closure. From the minutes of the SOS committee meetings, the request for funding came as a presentation delivered to the county commission by the committee. Several company employees, including the plant manager, were members of the committee and reported that nothing improper was discussed, since the donations were to be used for production and duplication of marketing materials, distribution of materials, further research on prospects, and recruitment activities to pursue qualified prospects.

Local press coverage was favorable: the donation was to help the committee find businesses to take over the closing plant or to hire employees:

> [The company] felt SOS had gotten to the point that they had done all the homework and needed a little extra help. The immediate need is to prepare brochures to send to potential companies. SOS Committee Coordinator said the money came just in time.

The SOS committee publicly thanked the company and Brent, who had helped to persuade the top staff to make the donation, because the contribution was the first to be made to the fund. Some plant employees were watching to learn if donations would be made from any other sources.

## Press Coverage

A local business magazine picked up the story of the plant closure and featured it as a cover story. One of the employees transferring to New Mexico was pictured on the cover, along with his family. The article spoke of this employee's dilemma in having recently finished his dream home in Utah, where the family planned to stay, and now facing a transition out of state. Though the employee's family considered the move an adventure, the employee still harbored some bitter feelings about it:

> [The company] was a missed opportunity. Apparently New Mexico did more for [the company] than Utah did. It's a step backward as far as this industry's concerned. Regardless of the reason for the shutdown, some politician could have hopped to it and helped [the company]. There was something that could have been done that wasn't. We're a premiere work force in Utah. We did all we could do. New Mexico has nothing over Utah, but maybe their government did more for them.

The article went on to say the plant was the largest property-tax payer in the city last year and the fourth-largest employer in the county. The closure would mean the loss of approximately $5 million in state and local taxes and around $38 million in payroll wages. Another employee was quoted as saying that he should have known something was up when the fab area that was promised new manufacturing equipment the previous year by corporate had its new equipment rerouted to the New Mexico plant. Since the employee featured in the article was one of the first of the engineering group to transfer, this succeeded in bringing into focus the impact of the closure on employees transferring with the company. Being forced to leave the state, albeit with a firm job, was causing real upheaval in some of the employees' personal lives. With some ninety families leaving the state, the shock waves would reverberate throughout the community for some time to come. Already the relocations had triggered a significant boom in the local real estate market, leaving a few well-connected real estate agents very busy and very rich.

At the end of June, the head count had dropped to around 820. In the past month, the number of people leaving had escalated because of release dates, transfers to New Mexico (around twenty-eight), and summer hiring from local businesses. Employees were typically not quitting voluntarily now, unless they had found other work lucrative enough to allow them to forfeit their completion bonuses. Those transferring in June to New Mexico were mainly engineers or technicians who had the critical skills needed in the fabrication area there. Anticipating the next month to be a pivotal time for turnover rates, each area in the plant was gearing up to deal with the transitions that inevitably occur when such a major change in head count takes place.

## Implications

### Maintain Realistic Expectations

Although most employees will behave ethically and follow their consciences in dealing with the company as they prepare to leave, management should not expect generally altruistic behavior. Employee work performance will clearly be negatively affected at some point. This is a time when employees at the plant will let down their guard to some degree and sometimes neglect their responsibilities at work. Although an initial instinctive reaction of management to any employee indiscretion is to clamp down hard and punish the offender, more can be accomplished through appealing to employees' sense of decency and integrity. By reminding employees of their obligations to coworkers and pointing out inappropriate behavior, the employee community will typically respond favorably in censuring this behavior. A strong employee community, which includes local management, can provide the requisite vigilance to ensure that unsuitable work behaviors will not proliferate.

### Recognize Good Performance

Management should celebrate outstanding performance up to the end, continuing to reinforce the importance of good work. Performance incentives and rewards beyond the typical severance pay should be considered. Even though at some point in the process employees will typically rechannel their energies away from work and toward reemployment, they will nevertheless respond to rewards and recognition for good performance. Employees will benefit from the attention and, through pride in their work, can rebuild self-esteem and self-worth. As we learned, it is not difficult for employees affected by downsizing to continue to work productively while searching for other employment; the best and most dedicated workers will maintain their excellent performance up to the end and still obtain some of the best employment opportunities when they leave. The company can regenerate trust and good will if it provides recognition to employees for their best work and at the same time reinforces to employees that their efforts at the plant are valuable.

The climate at the plant can be improved significantly if local management is allowed the freedom to sponsor recognition activities and involve employees in more meaningful ways in their work areas. The Utah plant had a team environment in many of the work areas already, so more empowerment was a natural step for these employees. There were some employees who were not interested or chose not to get directly involved in these initiatives, but we discovered most employees welcomed the opportunity to participate. The spirit of cooperation was contagious as teams planned everything from recognition activities to how they would run the work area during the closure period.

### Emphasize Community Relations

Community relations become even more important as employees prepare to make the transition to leave the plant. Donations to local community efforts in helping displaced workers will bolster morale and aid in spawning more community support services. Although some employees may express cynicism toward company donations for community-sponsored job search activities, these donations can help both to seed new business opportunities and to promote employee outplacement. If worker ownership is a viable enterprise for a closing plant, donations can advance these efforts and greatly reduce the adversarial feelings plant employees may harbor toward the company. If a local government search committee is formed, like the one in Utah, these financial contributions can make a difference in reemployment support, even if the loftier goal of finding a buyer and keeping the plant open is not attained. All the public advertisement and attention will draw interest to the plight of plant employees, increasing their opportunities to find other work.

### Consider On-Site Outplacement

An on-site outplacement center can provide the advantage of proximity and informality. It allows employees to wander in during breaks and lunches to peruse job postings or update résumés. Also, work groups can spend their downtime at the center engaged in productive job search strategies. The only way some employees will take advantage of an ouplacement center is to have a coworker accompany them. Obviously, funding and the size of the work force will be factors in determining whether on-site centers are feasible for companies.

### Coordinate Organizational Change

Sometimes parent company organizational changes can directly affect displaced plant employees. Many of the Utah plant engineering employees who received offers to relocate with the company were waiting to see what changes were afoot before they made their decisions. In this case, there were significant enough numbers of such employees to have strong impact on the company if they decided not to stay and relocate. Companies may want to take into consideration the effects of timing major organizational changes during a plant downsizing period.

# 9 July
## The Transitions Begin

In July, large numbers of employees started making transitions: employees in the engineering area were making the move to New Mexico; the beginning of the operations' phase-down period was triggering release dates; and the remaining employees were shifting gears to absorb the responsibilities of departing employees. In order to coordinate all the small department good-bye parties that were inevitable whenever a coworker left, most of the groups held one good-bye luncheon each month to include all employees from any department who were scheduled to leave that month. A sense of foreboding was present throughout the plant.

Those who had psychologically prepared themselves for the transition period seemed to be coping fairly well. Others who postponed plans and insulated themselves from this operation phase-down period began to panic. In spite of the forewarning in January, these employees had become victims of their own shortsightedness. One local physician, after having seen a number of patients from the company, commented that employees reported being under more stress; they perceived that the burden of responsibility was being shifted to them by managers and supervisors, who they claimed either weren't around much at the plant or no longer cared about what happened.

What determined whether or not an employee would adapt well under these circumstances and remain fully contributing until the end? Likewise, what characteristics turned a normally productive employee into a victim during this difficult time? The following stories should prove instructive.

Employee Transitions

One of the plant electronic engineers, who had accepted a position to transfer with the company to New Mexico, subsequently received an offer from another company in Utah. This particular engineer, Stan, had considerable software and hardware experience with the engineering group. The possibility of losing Stan caused much concern among the other transferring engineers. Stan was a rather shy and retiring individual, yet technically very capable. He was reluctant to discuss his dilemma with the other employees in his department. His family wanted desperately to stay in Utah, but he knew that the position he was offered from the other Utah company, a start-up operation, was not really what he wanted. His supervisor, Bill (a former university professor), was highly respected by many in the group including Stan and had some connections with the local air force base, where he had been contracted to do some software support work.

Bill approached Stan with the idea of joining him to do contract work, while still remaining with the company. This would enable Stan to make the transition to New Mexico, delay moving his family there, and turn down the other offer. Best of all, he would have a good connection in Utah should the family decide later not to move to New Mexico. Although this would extend the transition period for him and his family, Stan felt that this provided him with the insurance he needed to be able to make the move to New Mexico.

Another engineer in the group, Stewart, was similarly offered the opportunity to transfer to a position in New Mexico as a design engineer. Stewart, however, had not designed circuits for many years, having recently been functioning in a management-administrative position. Because of his lack of viable technical skills, Stewart was not included in the first round of offers that extended a two- to four-month incentive bonus to transfer to the New Mexico plant. When most of the experienced designers chose to leave the company, Stewart expressed interest in transferring and bid on one of the design positions. When Stewart later realized that he would not be given the relocation bonus, he pushed back. He discussed the matter with both the group engineering manager and group human resource manager in California to see if the bonus would be reconsidered for him. Unfortunately, the manager in California, Ben, had made a deal with the group human resource manager and the vice president that only the first-round offers would be considered for a bonus. Although he would have liked to have been able to offer this to Stewart, Ben could only express regret and maintain his firm position on the matter.

Stewart had not received other offers from companies in the industry because of his lack of hands-on technical design skills. He reluctantly accepted the offer from the company and proceeded to make arrangements to receive the necessary technical training to become a contributing design engineer. Because Stewart was paid well and had no family to support, the design manager, Jim, assumed that Stewart had come to terms with the situation. After several months passed, Stewart raised the issue of finances again with both Jim and human resources. Having recently returned from a house-hunting trip to New Mexico, Stewart claimed he was unable to make what he considered the financial sacrifices necessary to buy a home there. Once again he asked for additional financial consideration, adding that he was supporting both a mother and brother back East. Nevertheless, he received the same response from the company.

It became clear to those who knew Stewart that not being considered technically competent enough to be included with the group that received bonuses had damaged his pride. Although it appeared that he had dealt with this and was making the transition well into the individual contributor position, it was now evident that he was not. As the other engineers left one by one to go to other companies, Stewart was continually reminded of his private humiliation. Finally, after agonizing over the situation for some time, he announced that he had reconsidered and would not be able to accept the position to go to New Mexico. Later, Stewart confided that he had no idea what he would end up doing or where. His love for the outdoors and the surrounding environment in the West made it difficult for him to give all that up. He admitted that the New Mexico area was attractive and offered much of what he was looking for.

Tim was a manager in the fab manufacturing area who had previously worked in the New Mexico plant before transferring to Utah several years ago. He hoped the company would regard his previous stint in New Mexico favorably enough to make him an offer to transfer there again. As time passed and no offer came, Tim began to fear that his reputation may have been damaged by the events in the plant of 1990. Perceptions of the repressive management regime in the fab of which he was a part still existed. Although he could not substantiate his fears, Tim reconciled himself to looking outside the company for other work. He made contact with his former manager, now in Arizona, who quickly made him an offer. Suddenly, out of the blue, Tim received a call from the vice president of the division that included the New Mexico plant. Tim had worked for this man many years before when the vice president was an operations manager for one of the fab areas in the Utah plant. The phone call went something like this:

> VP:   Tim, why aren't you going to New Mexico to work for me there?
>
> Tim:  I kind of got the idea that no one was interested in me. I don't have an offer yet.
>
> VP:   Why didn't you call me and discuss this with me before? I hear you are considering leaving the company.
>
> Tim:  Well, I may be getting an offer from another company in Arizona. But my family and I would sure like to go to New Mexico instead.
>
> VP:   How committed are you to staying with the company and turning my fab area around down there?
>
> Tim:  If I get an offer from the plant down there, I would put my all into it.
>
> VP:   That's what I wanted to hear.

It wasn't long after the phone call that Tim received an offer from the New Mexico plant as the manufacturing manager in the newest state-of-the-art fab. He was convinced that the vice president had a hand in making this happen. In Tim's view, he had managed to pass a loyalty test the vice president or New Mexico plant management had devised. His transition period and relocation arrangements to New Mexico ended up benefiting both his family and the company, since the transfer of product from the Utah fab to the New Mexico fab was both problematic and prolonged. This transition period allowed his family to stay in Utah and sell their home, while Tim shuttled back and forth to Utah to work on the product transfer.

Sometimes the emotional roller coaster of trying to choose the best career move proved too stressful for certain employees. One such employee, Mitch, was caught up in this process for almost a year before the closure announcement. He had been the manager of one of the technical services groups for some time when the first reorganization took place. He was removed as the manager over the group and assigned a position as an individual contributor. Mitch never reconciled himself to being removed from the management position; he continued to maintain that it was a reorganizational error by the previous vice president of the division.

When the first-round offers to New Mexico went out to the technical services group, Mitch was not selected as a first-round choice. He lobbied hard with the design manager to whom he reported to create a position for him in the group that was transferring down. Meanwhile, Mitch granted himself considerable license in taking unaccounted time off to look for positions outside the company. His pride wounded, he balked when the hiring supervisor asked him to fill out a job bid form to apply for one of the positions in New Mexico (the first-round offers were done through original offer letters and not through the formal job bid system). When the design manager finally decided he could use Mitch's skills in the group, Mitch decided to play hard ball. He made a counteroffer, requesting that he receive all his severance and bonus pay prior to transferring. Furthermore, he requested that he be returned to his former management position with a significant salary increase and also required that several organization changes be made in the group with whom he would be working.

At this point, both the human resource and design managers felt that Mitch lacked perspective and only wanted to make an issue out of this with the company. Neither of them took the counteroffer seriously and told Mitch that they wished him well in his future career pursuits. Unfortunately, Mitch later revealed that he would have accepted the position without all of the conditions in his counteroffer. Mitch, torn by the thought of leaving the group, admitted, "I hate to leave all my friends and see them go down there without me." He later accepted a position outside the state and started negotiating for a quick release date.

Meanwhile, Mitch started having back problems, claiming to have injured his back while at work one day. Since his back seemed to be getting worse and he was reaching the end of his release period, he

discussed with the plant nurse the possibility of having his back surgery paid for by the plant. The nurse counseled him to be prudent
about the risks involved in surgery and convinced Mitch to try physical therapy for a while before venturing into surgery. But he became
vindictive when he learned that, according to plant policy, if he took
a medical leave (which he clearly wanted to do before leaving), he
might risk forfeiting his completion bonus. Nevertheless, having
been told by the insurance carrier that it would not support a workers' compensation claim to cover back surgery before the physical
therapy, Mitch capitulated. But as he departed on his last day, he left
the plant nurse with the impression that this might be one of the
more costly workers' compensation claims she had seen in a while,
because of the way he felt he had been victimized over the past year.

In the case of both Stan and Tim, the company's interest in working out an acceptable accommodation was influenced by the attitudes
of these employees. Both showed a willingness to take responsibility
for their situations, and each had a back-up plan in case the company
did not provide an acceptable offer. Further, both employees had developed and maintained important technical skills and experience
that made them more attractive to the company. Mitch and Stewart
had both allowed their value to the company to decline over the
years by failing to develop the necessary technical skills to stay competitive. Stewart was not motivated to update his design expertise
until he realized, too late, that these skills were the only way to ensure a lucrative enough offer to transfer with the company. Rather
than try and work out an acceptable compromise, Stewart became
insulted with his offer, withdrew, and then came back with a more
assertive demand. Mitch was even more aggressive and tried to take
advantage of the company with his offer demands and his diminish-
ing work ethic. Mitch didn't make any effort to take the company's
interest into consideration and instead blamed the company for his
predicament and became bitter and vindictive.

## Organizational Transitions

Since early 1992, the technical services organization had been under
the direction of three engineering managers, who in turn reported to
a division engineering manager in California. The manager in Califor-

nia, Ben, was highly regarded by all in the engineering group as a bright, capable, and honorable individual who said what he believed and acted accordingly. Thanks to his participative and cooperative style of management over the previous several years, Ben had won the loyalty and trust of nearly every engineer in the group, either through direct interaction or by reputation. Ben had managed to turn around one of the product groups that had been touted over the years as a proprietary, high-margin product group with a very poor performance record. That success made him a folk hero to the technical services group in Utah. He represented to them a long-awaited turning point in the division, renewing the success the division had experienced some years ago.

On a routine weekly visit to Utah, Ben drew the three engineering managers into an office to share with them his decision to leave the company. As they listened with shock and disbelief, Ben related to them the course of events that had forced him to make this decision. Having more than twenty years in the company, Ben had expressed his desire to the vice president to transfer as the engineering manager over the technical services group in New Mexico and retain his additional role as manager over the now profitable product group. He had been told by the vice president that this decision could not be made until the restructuring of the company was completed by the Dutch parent organization. When the outcome of the restructuring meetings became known the week before, Ben was told that he could no longer expect to retain the role as engineering manager as well as the product manager. Ben said he could not accept the diminished role now being offered him. The engineering managers relayed their concern about the impact Ben's leaving would have on the division.

Later that day, Ben confided to one of the managers that there was actually another more powerful reason why he could no longer stay with the company. His trust of the vice president had so eroded that he felt he could no longer work for him and still maintain the integrity in which he so strongly believed. Apparently, he had been asked by the vice president to compromise himself by sharing information that Ben believed was not accurate. When Ben had finally raised this issue the previous week with the vice president, he was told, "Oh, yeah. That trust thing. That's something the Japanese are good at." To further confirm his instincts, when Ben later informed the vice president of his decision to leave the company, the vice president asked Ben to not discuss his leaving with anyone in the organization but to go away quietly. The company would send out an e-mail announcement to the organization after the fact. It was evident that the vice president feared Ben's influence over key engineers could seriously jeopardize the company's recruiting and relocation efforts. Ben protested that he felt too much responsibility and personal obligation to the organization to do that to his people. He was able to convince the vice president to hold a group meeting a few weeks later to announce his leaving and to answer any questions the employees might have at that time.

When the day came for the official announcement of Ben's departure, the vice president came to the plant with Ben and another manager who would be later identified. Speculation was already intense within the technical service organization, since the vice president rarely visited the plant without a prepublished agenda. The vice president had no idea that Ben had ignored his instructions to refrain from telling anyone about his announcement. Ben advised the vice president that a question and answer period should follow the meeting, during which issues about the company could be addressed head on. Knowing that his departure would trigger more concerns about the company's stability and viability, Ben persuaded the vice president to help field the questions he knew would be asked.

In the meeting, Ben stood up first to address the group about his decision to leave the company. He shared the rationale that he was leaving for a better career opportunity (this he could say honestly) that would enable him to further develop his skills and experience. Thanking the group for their support and loyalty, Ben's voice became increasingly emotional. He turned the rest of the time over to the vice president and sat down.

The vice president emphasized how unhappy he was to see Ben leave and underscored the valuable contributions Ben had made to the company. The vice president spent the rest of the time providing data on how well things were going both for the division and the company overall. When the time came for questions, the first one was addressed to Ben: "Where are you going and is it spelled i-n-t-e-l?" Everyone laughed, recalling the group of design engineers who had recently joined that firm. Ben declined to say which company he was joining, but denied that it was Intel. Next came a question about the company, again addressed to Ben: "Do you know something about the company that we should know?" This suspicion resonated with many in the audience who continued to fear whether their decision to stay with the company and head to New Mexico was a good one. Ben reassured everyone that his decision to leave was not related in any way to company viability or performance. He stressed how impressed he had been with the division's performance of late and how the company would become even stronger as it aligned more closely with the parent company.

The final question focused on who would replace Ben in the division. At that point, the vice president introduced his visitor and indicated that this manager would be taking over part of Ben's product portfolio. Furthermore, a general announcement would be made on Friday, that would clarify the rest of the company organization, including Ben's direct replacement and the engineers' new boss. As the meeting closed, the engineers gave Ben a deafening round of applause. When the clapping stopped, one of the engineers paid Ben a final tribute: "You have won the respect and confidence of all of us, and we want to show our appreciation."

That afternoon, one of the more outspoken engineers, Alex, who had been ambivalent over his decision to go to New Mexico, spent some time with the vice president. He expressed anger and bitterness about Ben's departure and admitted that he and several other engineers were resigned to being too far into the relocation process to back out now. Alex lectured the vice president on the need for a cogent product plan to create some sense of direction for the engineers. He volunteered that the vice president himself was not liked or trusted by the group and predicted that the "new guy" (Ben's replacement) would have to do three things right to every one thing wrong just to survive.

When the organization announcement came that Friday, most of the employees viewed it as anticlimactic. The only surprise was the low-key approach in which the announcement in the plant was made. There were no meetings held, no general staff discussions, no e-mails transmitted. A faxed copy was distributed to the plant staff for them to share with anyone interested. The announcement went as follows:

As indicated during our recent employee communication meetings, the restructure program we have embarked upon includes the complete integration of [the company] into the [parent company division]. The purpose of the integration is to begin operating globally as a single entity with "one face to the customer." This change will result in a redistribution of authority to a lower level in the organization which will provide faster response to the marketplace. Two new organizational levels, namely Business Groups and Product Groups (MDPs), are being formed which will implement the structural change in our business. The result of these changes will be a strategically-oriented division addressing the key market segments in our mission statement, while maximizing the return on our total divisional asset base.

Attached to the announcement was an organizational chart indicating some changes of positions in the MDP units. The new managers named came predominately from the Dutch parent organization, additional confirmation that the company was eventually going to be run by the parent company. Also intimated in the announcement were further changes in the support organizations that pared back the corporate administrative structure and allowed the resources to become more decentralized.

## Relocation Transitions

Often, employee transitions can be largely invisible to the rest of the organization until there are physical signs of change. The technical services engineering organization now began that process. Offices were dismantled, desks shuffled around, and partitions removed; movers came to collect whatever was being shipped for the group going to New Mexico. The first five of the employees who were transferring left to relocate, including one of the managers. Another of the engineering managers, Jesse, who had made the decision to stay in Utah, found himself profoundly affected by all the changes. He ruminated over the demise of the engineering group of which he had been a part for the more than fifteen years since he began with the company. Looking very depressed and melancholy, Jesse said he had to get away from the area for a while. He promptly took some vacation days to allow himself time to adjust to the changes in the area.

Others in the group who planned to stay until their completion dates felt similarly. Many of them, resigned to the fact that they couldn't get any work accomplished during the dismantling phase, either chose to roll up their sleeves, put on jeans, and help the movers or to schedule time off to spend time with their families or pursue a job search.

The engineers transitioning to New Mexico were also affected by the dismantling of the area. Some attempted to get trained during this time by the remaining engineers. Several of these engineers, left with no functional equipment or trainers to do the training, were in limbo for a while. Others who were in transit between New Mexico and Utah and had little or no contact with their supervisors (including routine staff meetings), were left to speculate on rumors.

One of these rumors, likely triggered by Brent's trip to California to make a presentation to the top staff, was that the company had been sold. This rumor had been circulating around the plant for over a year, but gained new credibility when someone learned of Brent's trip. As it turned out, Brent was simply presenting a plan to sell the facility in Utah. He had recently escorted the realtors on a tour of the plant and had some information to pass on to corporate about the sale. From his meeting with the staff in California, Brent was able to influence both the president and the vice president of human resources to personally contact nine companies that were identified through the SOS committee as potential buyers of the Utah building.

When this plant rumor was cleared up, a new one took its place. Two of the design engineers were starting to panic over the possibility that their supervisor would decide not to transfer with the company after all. The supervisor, Jim, had been on vacation for a while and shortly afterward went to Europe on a business trip. The rumor was that Jim had reconsidered going to New Mexico and instead would be joining Intel with the other designers who had left. Since Jim was not around to dispel the rumor, had not yet moved his family to New Mexico, and had not identified a transfer date, the two designers felt the news must be true. They were all still recovering from the blow of Ben's announcement a few weeks earlier, and a feeling of uncertainty still hung over the group. When Jim returned from his trip and quickly denied the rumor, he was advised by another manager to identify his transfer date and then hold regular staff meetings in order to circumvent further speculation in the group. This helped to stabilize the transferring engineering organization.

Since Ben had left the company, the three engineering managers in the technical services organization, who were transferring to New Mexico, found themselves without an advocate. Stephen, Ray, and Jim were very different personalities with varied backgrounds. In particular, Jim and Stephen found themselves frequently at odds in their views of what needed to happen in the engineering organization. Jim suggested that, despite the leadership vacuum they were in, they ought to form a leadership team themselves and forge ahead. " After all," he offered, "we should act as if we own this business!"

That week they held an off-site meeting to make plans on how they felt the group should operate and decided to influence Ben's successor, a newly appointed Dutch Ph.D., to agree with their direction. At the meeting, Jim and Stephen aired their grievances and began to establish some rapport between themselves. When Hans, the Dutch manager, came to Utah that same week, they reported the plans they had formulated, which represented a surprisingly unified coalition. Hans found no reason, at that moment, to contest their plans and so encouraged them to continue their activities.

Hans, a very young and apparently bright protégé from the parent company, later met with human resources to get more information on both the managers and the organization. Asking for an organization chart of the group transferring to New Mexico, complete with names, positions, and manager, Hans looked into the backgrounds and styles of each of the three managers. Although he clearly had developed his own impressions, he sought corroboration in order to get a more complete picture of the group he had inherited. Admitting that he had some preconceived notions from the parent company of how the group should operate, Hans nonetheless seemed willing to wait and absorb all he could about the organization before imposing his own views on it.

One of the tasks facing the three engineering managers before transferring to New Mexico was clearing up all the delinquent property passes in their group. The Utah plant security manager was outraged when he discovered the laxity in the tracking system set up by his predecessor. There were over thirty delinquent property passes (which allowed employees to take equipment or company property off the premises) in the technical services organization alone. Fearful that transferring employees would leave the plant without returning company property, the security manager established a new property pass tracking system to ensure that accountability and reconciliation would take place before each departure. This proved to become a major issue for a few of the engineers who were using the equipment to do contract consulting work on the side. Nevertheless, with dogged determination and follow-through, all the delinquent property was located and finally returned to the plant.

Stephen, the first of the transferring engineering managers, was concerned about the inconsistencies in policy between the two plants. Not only did the New Mexico plant appear to have more restrictions on granting property passes, there were a number of plant cultural differences that affected the engineering group. The Utah plant policy was more liberal and less intrusive than the one they found in New Mexico. Back on a visit to Utah, Stephen enumerated the areas where differences might prove troublesome for the transferring group: no radios were allowed in the plant, including remotes for ham radios (these were pervasive in the Utah group); company badges were to be worn at all times; financial controls and policies were much more restrictive and bureaucratic; and employees were typically not allowed to come and go as they pleased with company computers. He foresaw that a task force would shortly be formed to look into the policy and culture differences between plants. He aimed to try to influence the New Mexico plant to loosen up on some of its controls for the benefit of the engineering group. Notwithstanding the frustration over the restrictive climate there, Stephen asserted that "if you want to stay with the company, it is clear that the New Mexico plant is the place to be."

Since the New Mexico plant was primarily a fab operation, those non-technical, production employees who didn't work in the Utah fab area and wanted to transfer were considered poor second choices for positions in New Mexico. The supervisors in the Utah assembly operation, some of whom had previous fab experience, resented what they felt was the cursory way they were treated by the hiring supervisors in New Mexico. In particular, three assembly supervisors desperately wanted to transfer. Seizing the opportunity created by the transfer of fab supervisors to New Mexico, these three supervisors asked for an opportunity to transfer to the local fab area to cover the vacancies made by these transferring fab supervisors. Their plan was to get current fab experience, in hopes that they would be considered viable candidates for future openings in New Mexico.

Attempting to represent her supervisors, Brenda intervened. She learned that the hiring supervisor in New Mexico had promoted two New Mexico plant employees with no previous supervisory experience to fill some of the positions instead of considering the three Utah assembly supervisors for the same positions. Brenda called to discuss the matter with both human resources and Brent, asking them to look into the matter further. After she tried on several occasions to contact the hiring supervisor in New Mexico, with no response, she decided to make it an issue that required formal investigation. After reviewing the matter, the human resource manager in Utah discovered that no one had ever bothered to follow up with these three supervisors to tell them why they were not selected. According to them, after they were interviewed, the next thing they knew, the positions had been filled.

"I don't want to ram my people down their throats, but aren't they entitled to some feedback here?" Brenda queried. "I feel like no one wants to give me or them a straight answer. I will pursue this until I get a satisfactory response." She finally heard from the New Mexico human resource manager that their plant management felt no obligation to give first consideration to displaced Utah employees over its own employees. The New Mexico manager indicated that the two people who filled the positions did have some previous supervisory experience (not with the company) and were being groomed to move into the positions as a career step. The manager reassured Brenda that the three assembly supervisors would be considered for future positions that would probably open up in the fall.

Managing all the relocation transition concerns and problems can be a formidable task if a healthy contingent of employees are transferring to other company sites. Fortunately, management at the New Mexico plant was generally supportive in helping to manage these transitions. A task force composed of Utah and New Mexico managers was created to look into policy and procedure issues affecting the relocating employees. Efforts were made to try and match hiring needs at the New Mexico plant with interested displaced Utah employees. Despite Brenda's best efforts, none of the three assembly supervisors ended up finding positions within the company. Some of the employees who didn't get positions felt the New Mexico managers had been disingenuous with them, but they later found other work and left determined to make the best of it.

## Outside Recruitment

When the outplacement center was first announced, many employees formed the impression that during the summer months, there would be job fairs sponsored by the on-site center for companies that were recruiting plant employees. This had not yet happened. Finally, word got out that a California semiconductor company was attempting to arrange for an on-site visit. This company wished to hold interviews with interested employees in the plant. Phone calls were made by the center to the respective human resource representatives to plan the logistics of the visit. Initially, the plant staff was reluctant to grant the visit at the time requested, since the fab operation was still trying to induce engineers to stay through their release dates. Because engineers were the target of the recruiting effort, it appeared to them that the company was doing them a disservice rather than accommodating their outplacement needs. When the engineers complained, the problem suddenly became a flap that escalated to the vice presidential level at both companies.

The companies agreed on a recruiting visit date, and the recruiting company committed to discuss openly all intended offers before extending them to the employees. This would enable the company to negotiate release dates for the selected employees with the new employer, rather then to lose them through a normal recruiting process. The California company agreed to the plant's terms, since this provided wider access to the employees and allowed it to focus its recruiting in one area. Fortunately, what could have become an employee relations nightmare turned out to be a win-win situation for all.

More recruiting support could have occurred if the outplacement center had been allowed free rein to manage this process. Many more companies than were allowed to recruit tried to arrange to come into the plant. Unfortunately, corporate management was afraid that key employees would be lured away before they had fully completed their assigned tasks. This engendered some bitterness among the most sought after engineers who were recruitment targets. Most claimed that they would have bargained with potential employers to seek accommodations so they could stay until their release dates and earn their completion and severance bonuses.

## Employee Communications

The company president returned for his quarterly employee communications meeting. Because of the small numbers in attendance, interest in company affairs appeared to be waning. First, Brent made some general announcements on the progress to sell the building. Then he reviewed the rate of use for the outplacement center, gave an SOS committee update, and went over the performance numbers for each operation area. The division vice president gave an update on how the division performed the first half of the year and admitted that the increase in business sales had helped considerably toward achieving profitability. He predicted a profit of around $14.5 million for the division by the end of the year (the plant performance was rolled up into this particular division).

When the president's turn came, his first announcement was addressed directly to the employees:

> I'm not surprised but pleased by your good performance for the first six months of this year despite the personal burden that you are all carrying. I'm appreciative of this, as is [parent company], since [company] right now is carrying the rest of the semiconductor divisions for the present. The Utah plant is a highly visible entity for [parent company] and does not go unnoticed.

When the time came for questions, only a few employees volunteered any, and most of these were mundane. As he closed the meeting, the president delivered a message to employees working in the fab area, which remained the largest of the plant operations. Promising to stage a celebration when the manufacturing cost of a wafer fell below the $100 mark, the president ended the meeting. This promise stunned and silenced the crowd of employees. Murmuring over their reactions, the fab employees immediately, on returning to the plant, proceeded to share with their coworkers their perception that this message was a slap in the face. Most felt they were already giving their best efforts and resented the carrot they believed the president was trying to dangle in front of them. "Haven't we given enough already?" was their response to the president's perceived challenge.

One of the fab managers shared her own feelings after listening to the highly emotional reactions of her employees: "Why does he continue to hold these meetings here when all they serve to do is to stir people up? Employees don't care about how the company is doing; they want recognition for *their* efforts! My graveyard people were already upset about not getting paid to come in and attend these meetings. What these people need is meaningful feedback and information." Taylor was even more disturbed by the president's supposed challenge to the fab. Since his group was chartered with the main responsibility for fab yields, he took the president's comment personally: "I can't believe he expects us to do more than we already have despite the obstacles we're facing. I'm lucky to have managed to retain the key engineers that I have—and I'm going to be doing some unorthodox things to try and hold on to those who have other jobs and will be quitting." Taylor was able to strike some deals with human resources to retain his key engineers by creating some flexible work schedule arrangements that benefited both the fab operation and the individual engineer.

Needless to say, Utah managers were against having the company president hold more communication meetings. The circle of concern and influence in the plant had narrowed to the extent that team meetings were now the only kind of meeting the employees found worthwhile.

## Productivity Concerns

In the wake of the fab productivity problems, certain areas of the assembly operation were now being affected by slipping performance and apathy. One of the managers in the quality department began seeking out ideas on how to deal with the problem and prevent further impact on the operation. His dilemma was whether or not to confront the problem directly with the employees or indirectly through positive morale-building activities. Poor quality, lowered productivity, and some apparently isolated cases of theft (including $500 from a petty cash fund) were among the problems that management felt needed to be addressed. With the three long-term assembly supervisors transferring to fab, and even less supervisor loyalty, many employees seemed not as concerned with the results of their work. One employee, two weeks away from exiting, paid so little attention to his work that the area ended up throwing away everything this employee did during that time.

John, the quality manager, reported pressure from corporate to eliminate the petty cash funds and impose stronger controls in the area. Reluctant to take such drastic measures, John hoped for a more positive solution. The fab experience from a month ago proved instructive to this area. Rather than assume a general problem shared by all employees, John was advised to identify specific causes and to deal directly with the employees involved. John agreed that the more low-key approach made sense and also avoided the risk of alienating those employees who were still giving their best efforts.

### Employee Retaliation

Surprisingly, there had been few cases of horseplay and retaliatory pranks against the company since the closure announcement. One manager, who was on the plant closure steering committee and had been involved with retrofitting the plant to comply with the safety code, confided that he had recently been a victim of employee retaliation. He speculated that his highly visible involvement in getting the plant up to code led an employee to assume that he also played a role in the decision to close the plant. Someone (he suspected one of his own subordinates) had been pouring water into his car's gas tank. He had also been the subject of a recently submitted poem in a plant limerick contest, which linked him to the decision to close the plant. This incident reinforced the suspicion that many employees were either still unclear about the reasons behind the plant closure, or they were simply not buying into the rationale given them by management.

The plant limerick contest, one of the devices used to promote plant morale and advertise the company's annual employee summer get-together, signaled some continuing employee animosity. As it

turned out, the subject of over half of the limericks submitted by
employees was the plant closure. Most were humorous and good-
natured, but some showed no attempt to disguise bitterness:

> We were once a fine group called Signetics
> Who, of late, had turned into frenetics
> For our future looked dim;
> Rumor's true, announced Jim [company president]
> Now we're practicing job search kinetics.

> To Utah, did Jim once again venture
> And our mirth about ISO (audit) did censure;
> The plant staff feared discord . . .
> Said 'a sundae's no reward . . .
> This plant needs a summer adventure.

> Jim spoke to us at the Scera
> The irony couldn't be cleara
> For the ISO we got
> A kick in the butt
> Now our 60 day notice is neara.

> I see no irony here
> Said Jim with a sneer
> On this point you see
> We just disagree
> But Signetics has no audits to fear.

> Signetics has been quite a gas
> The managers really have class
> They say we've exceeded
> The performance they needed
> So now we'll be laid off en mass.

> So Signetics is closing, I hear. . .
> Is all that I've heard for a year
> From my mom and my pop
> My neighbor, a cop
> It won't ever stop, so I fear.

Some employees still carried grudges toward the company in general and the company president in particular. Those who continued to harbor ill feelings appeared to have a more difficult time making a successful transition. As they left, the employees who saw the closure as an opportunity to move on and do something proactive with their careers were the ones who stayed positive and upbeat. Employees who had never quite come to terms with the closure and resented its disruption of their lives continued to suffer, emotionally and in some cases professionally.

## Implications

### Plan for Contingencies

As transitions begin at the plant, with employees leaving and work groups getting dismantled, employees can easily slip back into despair and resignation. Unless they make preparations to accept such passages and insulate themselves with their own career plans, employees can wind up feeling deserted both by the company and their coworkers. If, however, employees are following a carefully prepared plan that includes contingencies, the transition period need not be so stressful. Nevertheless, it is difficult to watch the demise of community within the plant and the elimination of a strong support system. By replacing that support system with contacts and ties outside the plant, employees can make their own transitions with some confidence.

### Balance Interests

Employees who are the most successful in obtaining job offers, either from the company or other sources, typically find ways of keeping both parties' interests in mind. Rather than becoming victims of their circumstances, they find ways to generate creative options and take responsibility for doing what is necessary to stay competitive in their professions. These employees tend to be more proactive and do not dwell on what has happened in the past.

Although company loyalty can be a positive force, it should not be a significant factor in making career decisions. Utah employees who tended to base their relocation decisions mainly on what happened to certain managers or on division changes, were prone to disappointment as the managers subsequently moved on and the expected changes never materialized. Employees must face their employment decisions with the knowledge that the only controllable variable under the circumstances is their own attitude.

Managers must recognize that as production begins to wind down and employees start to leave the plant, any psychological ties that remain among employees will be in work groups and work areas, not with the plant or the company. Company loyalty cannot be counted on to motivate employees to work hard and do the right things toward the end. Employees will respond to those in the company who they believe have treated them justly and fairly. Supervisors can help foster loyalty by tailoring outplacement services to the specific needs of their employees. By explaining and encouraging the use of these services, supervisors and managers can generate a smoother transition period.

### Allow Autonomy

At this point in the downsizing process, the company should provide as much autonomy and control to specific work areas as possible. Allow latitude for work areas to manage as they need to as employees begin to leave and they make arrangements for remaining employees to cover. Local managers who will ultimately be leaving the company must feel they have control to keep areas running and attend to their worker's needs. First-line supervisors in the closing plant now become essential to ensuring that the closure process will proceed as intended. These key employees must not only attend to the areas' work needs but must keep themselves and their people productive, all this at the time when they face their own anxieties about reemployment.

### Plan for Productivity

Retention packages should be planned with productivity in mind, yet work conditions at this time can become a more critical factor. If other job offers become available to local managers and they feel they do not have the necessary control and trust they need to accomplish their goals, they may not remain until the end, despite incentives. Companies will often attempt to exert tighter control toward the end, perhaps even bringing in management teams from other company sites. By allowing the plant supervisors to deal with work and productivity issues as they deem appropriate, however, the company can avoid inadvertently causing plant employees to feel that they are not to be trusted. Typically, each production area will have a good idea as to the cause of any specific problems that may occur and can discreetly handle situations without upsetting the entire work area. If trust and confidence in local management continues, plant employees will usually accomplish what is necessary to run operations and maintain plant morale at the same time. More is attained through trust and leniency at this time than through intervention.

### Continue Outplacement Investment

Policymakers should avoid making outplacement service decisions with the same cost-effectiveness criteria followed under normal business circumstances. This is a time when most of these services will be tested and used by displaced employees, although they may have been available previously. Employees will often procrastinate taking advantage of these services until the need becomes more obvious and immediate. If these services have been pared back or phased out due to initial lack of interest, both the employees and the company will suffer from the ensuing backlash of panicked job seekers. The press will now resume a strong interest in the closure, and public relations may take a real bruising if the transition process doesn't occur as smoothly as possible.

Stage 7: Transitions

| Employees | Management | Policymakers |
|---|---|---|
| —Take advantage of services provided<br>—Prepare for departures of friends and coworkers<br>—Avoid complacency<br>—Be engaged in career plans and new skill acquisition | —Help manage and encourage use of outplacement services<br>—Tailor services to specific needs<br>—Make work rearrangements to cover operations and cross-train employees | —Provide adequate outplacement services<br>—Allow flexibility in operation coverage<br>—Concentrate on community and public relations support |

# 10 August
## The First Domino Falls

When the time finally arrives for a long-awaited event to occur, two reactions typically follow: a feeling of relief that the time has finally arrived or a feeling of disappointment as the event turns out to be anticlimactic. The latter was the case for many of the employees in the technical services organization as shutdown time came for that operation. Part of the reason for this feeling was that a small crew of around twenty people would remain in the plant through December to support the transfer team. Since the bulk of this operation was transferring to New Mexico, there was also less of a feeling that work was coming to an end. Still, a certain sadness hung over the group as final arrangements were made to transfer people and equipment to New Mexico.

Many employees in the technical services group, having worked together for more than ten years, had forged strong bonds. Several had maintained close associations with coworkers who had left the organization, creating a rich network of job contacts to ply. A few had started up their own engineering consulting businesses with former employees and negotiated contracts with the company to continue providing services to the New Mexico plant. Quite a number of creative employee business ventures had been considered or attempted.

## Granting Extensions

The first dilemma facing the plant, now that this technical services group was disappearing, was to bridge the work gaps that became evident as people left. Release dates were formally assigned to employees based on projected needs for certain skills and support levels. As it turned out, many of the dates were realistic and on target. Others, however, fell short of the actual need. The technical services group had overoptimistically calculated their release dates, believing that staffing needs would be met. This was an attempt to benefit the employee, who by that time might have found other employment and would desire to leave earlier than later. Counting on the fallback strategy to grant extension letters to employees who were needed longer, group managers saw no reason for concern about the accuracy of release dates. Problems began, however, when the first set of employee extension requests for that group were made.

Rumors started in the plant that employees in the technical services group were getting special deals again. Responding to these charges, Brent asked about the specific circumstances behind the extensions. He reflected his own concerns regarding the perception that employees who received early release dates and subsequently an extension could then function as free agents, receiving their completion bonus and being allowed effectively to work until the closing or until they chose to leave. This put the control not with the operational areas but with the employee.

As a rebuttal to these concerns, the technical services managers countered the assumption that employees were doing all the initiating or negotiating of their extensions. In some instances this might have applied, but it was the exception and not the rule. Furthermore, they maintained that employee extensions were for legitimate business reasons and were intended as win-win solutions in situations in which the original release dates were not set accurately. Finally, they pointed out that the extension letters did not guarantee the employee work up to a certain date, but only projected a date in the future that could not be exceeded.

As a concession, the technical services group finally agreed to have the plant staff review all employee extensions beyond one month before they were granted. Everyone agreed that by being more open about their plans, the technical services area would be less susceptible to charges of unfair practices by other employees. Sometimes the fear of what employees would perceive as unfair practices in the plant became so pervasive that it clouded judgment in a given area. The danger was in becoming too inflexible and prescribing policies for every little wrinkle that appeared on the closure horizon. Ironically, the group had been previously perceived as being too willing to allow employees to negotiate their release dates and leave early, but now feelings were that the group was accommodating extensions to allow employees to stay on and work longer.

## Recalling Company Equipment

Because of the large number of employees in the technical services operation leaving in August, exit interviews were held in groups rather than individually. One of the issues yet to be resolved was the property pass delinquencies for exiting people. Normally, all passes had to be reconciled with security and all equipment returned before the employee's last day. During the group exit, it became clear that several employees still had equipment and had no plans to return it in the near future. They apparently had been led to believe that their supervisor, Bill, had made the necessary arrangements to allow for them to continue using the equipment in a contract agreement. When informed that no such agreement had been made, they reluctantly submitted to a request by security that they either return the equipment immediately or make arrangements to do so in the near future. As he left his final exit interview, one engineer commented, "These security types have no sense of humor."

Further investigation determined that the supervisor, Bill, had signed out five computer systems to former employees until February 1993. Further, several of the signatures on the property passes appeared to be forged. At this point, Brent and the controller got involved. Rumors escalated that Bill, who had signed out the equipment, did not intend to transfer to New Mexico after all but was instead venturing into a local software support business. When the manager of this group, now located in the New Mexico plant, was asked about what he knew of this, he pleaded ignorance. The manager asked Bill to take charge of clearing this issue up with security and plant management by the end of the week. Part of the issue concerned which equipment was designated to transfer to the New Mexico plant and which was identified as surplus. Surplus equipment could be sold legitimately to the employees for their personal use.

Further complicating the matter was the fact that the equipment contained proprietary software and designs, which potentially could be used by the employees for other companies and thereby violate a nondisclosure legal agreement that each employee had signed. The legal department was asked to help draft an agreement to deal with both the use of the equipment and software and to ensure full disclosure on intent for the use of each. Brent informed Bill that his interest was not to obstruct unnecessarily the software venture, but rather to ensure that everything was above board and agreed to in advance by the company. Bill's inherent distrust of management and company policy seemed to get in the way of what could have been a much more straightforward process. No quick resolution was imminent.

With the technical services operation shutting down, the New Mexico plant became interested in what equipment and materials might be available for transfer. New Mexico management requested a plant inventory list and any items deemed surplus that normally would be made available for employee purchase. By applying leverage to the plant staff to give the New Mexico plant first consideration before offering items for sale, the human resource manager in New Mexico made it clear that that plant's resource needs should be paramount. The Utah plant controller and materials manager began to itemize excess equipment, both to comply with this request and in preparation for the employee sale to be held the next month.

## Relocating Employees

Both material resources and human resources appeared to be up for grabs by the company product groups that were recently formed by the parent company. These groups were demanding total control over the technical people who were supporting their projects, including budget and head count control. Normally, the technical groups were organized by functional discipline and reported to a technical manager who had the same background and skill base. This provided both economies of scale for the organization as well as solid technical leadership in the group. The employees recently transferred from the Utah plant to New Mexico in technical services were disturbed by the impending reorganization, which they perceived would leave their group fractured and disjointed. The ripple effect of this change was difficult to predict, yet it appeared that several recently transferred engineers were making contingency plans to leave the company if their concerns were not addressed.

Although this problem was only one of several transition-related issues involving employees who were relocating to New Mexico, there was a clear need to address some of the issues more proactively. A meeting was scheduled in New Mexico to present some concepts on cultural change and transition management and also to identify other topics that might present similar conflicts. The feedback from this meeting made it clear that many employees were still in upheaval from the move. During this transition period, these issues—however minor and petty—were creating big ripples in the organization, since employees still felt unsettled and apprehensive about the move in general. Emotions were close to the surface, and any incremental problems added disproportionately to levels of stress.

Adding to the perception that the two plants had very different practices and cultures, the results of a recently administered survey were discussed with both the transferees and the local plant staff. An organizational profile showed the Utah group as a highly supportive and innovative community. In contrast, the New Mexico plant profile showed a highly bureaucratic organization that scored low on innovation. The New Mexico plant staff was invited to review and consider the data as part of their cultural issues team process. Among the Utah relocatees, hope glimmered that the New Mexico plant might make accommodations to address some of the more troublesome differences.

Another organizational issue for the transferring technical services group had recently become evident, particularly for the design group. Jim had expected that in his role as design manager for the technical services organization, he would retain authority and control for the entire design resources. He had been told by the division vice president to whom he reported that although there was pressure from the parent company to break up the design resources by product group, the vice president would keep the group intact for at least six months. In a meeting with the product group managers, however, Jim learned that this structure *would* change: the design employees would be divided by product and would report directly to each of the product groups. Feeling betrayed and shocked by this news, Jim confronted the vice president, who told him that his hand had been forced on this matter, adding, "We need to figure out what we do with you now."

Devastated by this turn of events, Jim contemplated what recourse remained. He wondered if he could claim that this role change constituted a breach of contract of his original offer and subsequent acceptance. After hearing about this change and fearing the worst, several of the designers panicked at the possibility of losing Jim, who was highly esteemed by his people. Jim had not yet relocated his family to New Mexico, a factor that would make it easier for him to call it quits. Coached by one of the managers and supported by his two counterparts, Jim decided first to negotiate with one of the local product group managers. His proposal to help provide functional leadership to the design group was accepted; in addition, he would retain his role in logic design management. This prompted Jim to stay with the company for the moment. But he remained apprehensive about further structural changes originating from the parent company.

## Plant Communications

In the monthly Utah plant employee communications meetings, Brent polled each shift to find out how many of the employees still cared or wanted to hear about company statistics. Only those on day-shift indicated continuing interest in the numbers. The company reported a loss of around $3 million year-to-date, although the previous several months had been profitable. In light of a budgeted loss of $14 million, this was a significant turning point for the company. Under normal circumstances, this would have evoked a cheer from the employee audience. Needless to say, the reaction now was less than enthusiastic. The plant head count had decreased from 930 in January to 770 in August. Of the employees who had left, 71 percent reported finding other work.

Several of the questions posed in the question-and-answer portion of the meeting still reflected a sense of dissatisfaction with some of the company benefits. One employee asked why the total amount budgeted for retraining benefits couldn't simply be divided up equally among all employees and distributed for use toward degree programs. Another employee, apparently a contract temporary, asked why the plant couldn't just hire all temporaries as full-time employees and provide them with benefits until the end of the year. This employee claimed that a real status differential in the fab area made it difficult for the temporaries to integrate successfully into the teams.

Brent's response to these questions was both sensitive and diplomatic:

> There are reasons why we were able to get approval to provide retraining benefits to employees and hire temporary workers this year. There were certain assumptions built into our proposals and the conditions under which these budgets were approved. If we violate those agreements or terms, it is likely that the monies will no longer be available to us. Hopefully we were forthright with all of you concerning the terms of those benefits and your employment. We will continue looking at what makes sense for both the company and the employees. Being a temporary should not prevent you from working together effectively as a team. At this point we are all temporary employees.

The vice president had arrived that day to present the division's results to all interested employees. This meeting followed the day-shift employee communication meeting. Normally, his presentations attracted a large gathering, but only fourteen people showed up this time. Those attending speculated that this was partly due to the general lack of interest in company performance and partly to the dislike and, in some cases, animosity employees felt for this man, who had become a symbol of the insensitivity and callousness of company management toward the Utah employees.

## Symbols of Impending Closure

On our arrival at work one morning in the second week of August, a change greeted us at one of the entrances to the building. A For Sale sign had just been placed in plain view for everyone to see. One of the managers, on seeing the sign, went directly to Brent to express his concern about potential repercussions to morale. The receptionist stationed at the door that day relayed the comments she had received from employees as they entered after seeing the sign for the first time. A typical response she heard was "Well, I guess this makes it all nice and official." Strangely enough, some of the employees who entered the building at another entrance expressed dismay that they didn't get a sign for their doorway. Brent, who had been involved with the SOS committee in selecting a realtor, received so many complaints about the sign that he finally started offering the following advice to employees: "Those employees who want to see the sign, go through the west entrance. Those that don't want to see it, enter through the east doors."

There was general confusion among employees and the local community about the role of the SOS committee in selling the building. An update from the committee attempted to clarify the contacts:

> It should be noted that the SOS mission focuses on the labor force while [local realtor] has been retained to market the facility. While the goals of the two organizations are not the same, they are complementary. Our objective is to attempt to find a company that could utilize the expertise of the existing [company] labor force. The SOS group is pleased to have another entity working to find a buyer for the facility.

At the rate employees were finding jobs and leaving the company (even as most were waiting through their sixty-day notice period), SOS would have to scramble to keep much of a labor force intact when and if the time came that an interested buyer was found.

## Job Networking and Outplacement

Although the outplacement center had proven helpful to many of the employees in getting job leads, most of the real job finds had come through networking with previous employees. Brenda was surprised to find that she had such a contact through the former vice president who had left the company over a year ago. She received a call for a job interview from one of the larger local employers who had recently hired this vice president. After interviewing favorably and receiving the job offer, she mused over the way the contact had been established: "I really am amazed that he [vice president] would have known enough about me to have made the recommendation. All I can imagine is that he must have remembered one of the presentations I did for the corporate staff on some of the work we were doing in assembly. I certainly didn't have a lot of contact with him directly outside of that."

Brenda was delighted with the offer and was able to work out an arrangement with the plant staff that she continue working until her completion date, while starting part time at her new job. After all her efforts to remain productive and a positive example in her area, the plant staff was more than happy to accommodate her. She recognized that for the next month she would be required to put in close to sixty-hour work weeks, but was eager to start in her new environment. Unfortunately, she did not anticipate the backlash from some of her coworkers who had also applied to work at the same company. Two of her employees accused her of taking the job they had applied for and not telling them about it. They felt she had both brown-nosed her way to the former vice president and taken credit for the work they had done in assembly. Stung by these accusations, Brenda tried to defend herself. Her sincerity convinced the two employees that her motives were pure, but they resented her nonetheless for landing the coveted job which they themselves desired.

Several of the fab operators on graveyard had complained about not being able to access the outplacement center on their shift. Although the center was open at six a.m. a few mornings a week, they lobbied for extended hours. The plant management was reluctant to do this because of the additional cost involved and because of a similar experience with the cafeteria hours. Responding to the graveyard's protests that they were not able to influence cafeteria hours, the staff decided to extend the hours of the cafeteria during graveyard on a trial basis. When the statistics showed that the usage had not changed enough to warrant extended hours, the cafeteria had gone back to its previous schedule. The plant staff decided that if graveyard employees were serious enough about their job search, they would make the necessary arrangements to get to the center during the hours it was open.

In fact, when it became evident that the hours were not going to change, the graveyard employees most serious about job hunting did find ways to access the center. The rest chose to either not use the center or wait until their completion dates, when personal schedules would permit more flexibility. The message that the center needed to be more customer-oriented, however, did get across. A steering committee was formed of employees from each area of the plant to ensure that employee concerns were registered and followed up on. The result was more local job postings, express services for résumés (for interviews), and an on-line job listing bulletin board.

## Productivity Initiatives

Fab managers reported that it was increasingly difficult to keep their employees upbeat and focused on their work. Many were still experiencing great stress and anxiety over their impending job loss. The teams in the fab were now working on team-building activities to enhance the support structure and allow employees to discuss the pressures and stress they were feeling. Some normally minor issues tended to get blown out of proportion on the teams, as defenses went up and emotions rose to the surface.

One of the associated problems facing the fab was lower attendance, particularly on the weekends when overtime was required. In an attempt to be creative in finding incentives to increase weekend attendance, one fab team, along with the supervisor, proposed an incentive pay program. This proposal, purely a grassroots effort, was pitched to the division vice president while he was visiting this month. Taken by surprise, the plant staff and the vice president reacted defensively and called the plan half-baked. The proposal began with the following prediction:

> There Are Only Two Options; 1. Schedule is missed by 4,838 wafers, or 2. Eight fully productive overtime days are worked by December 15.
> We do not recommend mandatory overtime due to decreased worker morale and productivity, decreased yields, increased absenteeism, and increased cycle time. We are shutting down, the people will not support us if we work them to death—there is no incentive for them.

Essential features of the proposal included double time pay versus the standard time-and-a-half pay, a $50 bonus for each Saturday worked, another $50 bonus for perfect attendance two weeks preceding the overtime worked, and a $50 bonus for each period when the schedule goals were met. The cost of the program was estimated at $508,000—not a paltry figure even in the best of circumstances.

Since plant management wasn't sure about the plan, the supervisor of the team that devised it was instructed to take it back to the team to rethink the rationale, the costs, and the approach. Afterward, the vice president revealed his skepticism of pay incentive plans. He believed that when people's basic security needs are not being met, pay is not a motivator. Nonetheless, the team was determined to follow through, hoping that some form of the proposal might get approved. When the news reached the fab that the first proposal had been rejected, there was a lot of grousing about how it took forever to get anything approved through the proper channels. Given the urgency to get something implemented quickly, the team worked with the fab management and the plant staff to move through the bureaucracy and revamp the proposal, with the support of plant management. Brent agreed to help the effort and champion the cause of getting a plant incentive plan presented and approved through the corporate staff during his next trip to California headquarters.

Because this productivity plan was a team-based initiative, it was not greeted with the suspicion that a management proposal would have received. Realizing that such a plan would be successful only if it was beneficial to and supported by all employees, plant management was careful to share this proposal with the entire plant.

Shutdown Crews

As operations started to wind down, employee interest in getting on the closure cleanup crew peaked. Several months before, it had been decided that a crew of 100 to 140 people would be responsible for the equipment and facilities cleanup, disposition, and restoration. The crew would remain into 1993 for as long as it took to complete the closure tasks. Members of this crew would receive their sixty-day notice for 15 December, making them eligible for their severance and completion bonus. They would each then receive an offer to stay and work voluntarily for as long as they wished until the completion of the work. This effectively allowed those employees on the crew to become free agents and find other work while they remained at the company.

More employee interest than was originally anticipated had made the selection process problematic. The plant staff used time to retirement, company anniversary dates (which affect the amount of severance pay), and relevant task skills as the criterion for the selection of more than 250 interested candidates. The purpose of the crew selection evolved from one of ensuring that the right mix of people and skills were included to one of providing a mechanism to retain key people through the end of the year. One of the fab managers pressed hard to include three of his supervisors on the crew in order to secure their retention through December. Because of the crucial nature of the role of the supervisor in maintaining the morale and climate of the fab area, particularly as outside job opportunities became more available, this request was approved, and the three were added to the list.

Once they were informed that they had made it on the crew, the employees who were staying into 1993 asked if they would be considered for a merit increase (normally held in March for the past year's performance). Since the plant manager's input on this matter would carry considerable weight with corporate management, Brent deliberated about the implications of this decision. He reviewed the appropriateness of using a merit increase as an additional pay incentive, which would act as a sizable kicker in the calculation of severance and completion bonus for those who received it. Given the fact that some of the managers, including himself, were staying into 1993 to help shut down the plant (their completion dates were targeted for April 1993), he could argue to grant a normal merit increase to those few people. Since these managers did not have the flexibility that the closure crew was given to collect their bonus and leave at any time in 1993, Brent was reluctant to also provide the crew with the same financial benefit.

On the other hand, Brent knew full well the repercussions if it became known to the crew that only the management team would receive merit increases. Many of the crew would likely still be around in March when the increases would be granted. For the moment, Brent decided to defer making a recommendation until the end of the year. At that time, the administrative support processes available to the plant would be clearer, as would the reaction of the remaining employees to this issue.

## Operations Coverage

As some of the key technical employees left for other jobs, employees in those departments were asked to fill in and take over the responsibilities of their coworkers. In some cases, this resulted in career opportunities and job promotions for those assuming the new responsibilities. For other employees who already had the relevant skills and had previously performed the job duties, however, no salary increase seemed warranted. Yet some employees—resentful of being asked to do more for a few months before the closure—had attempted to hold their work for ransom, demanding that their pay be adjusted up. This posed a real dilemma to the company, since many other employees, willing to help out, had absorbed the additional load without complaint or resentment. The company was left with two choices: provide the incentive pay or resort to negative sanctions (such as corrective action) to get the employee to comply with the work request.

Attempting to remain consistent on the rules for promotions and adjustments, the company resisted management requests for pay increases only for employees who otherwise would not do the work. In one case, a manager over the engineering department in electrical sort operations tried to justify adjusting the pay of an engineer who was covering for another departing engineer. This engineer had recently received a pay increase and was being paid at a fair market rate. Because he did not honor the request that he take over the duties of the other engineer, the manager felt that his only recourse was to provide a pay increase. When human resources pushed back on the adjustment, the manager went back to his operations manager to discuss strategy. By changing the job code and adding responsibilities that crossed over shift boundaries, they ultimately contrived a rationale that this new assignment was indeed an organizational promotion. The promotion went through when the manager was able to convince one of the human resource representatives of its legitimacy.


## Ongoing Politics

Corporate headquarters had just announced other organizational changes that affected mainly the New Mexico and California operations. One change in human resources seemed to portend a move of company headquarters from California to New Mexico.

The person who replaced the human resource development manager, who would be retiring in October, worked at the New Mexico plant. Also named as the new head of human resource operations was the current group human resource manager, Rex, who was responsible for supporting the division to which the New Mexico plant reported. His counterpart, a more senior and seasoned manager (whom many had expected to move up into this position), was left with less responsibility than he currently had. Some speculated that the more senior manager had burned too many bridges with the ascending division vice president responsible for the New Mexico plant. Russell, this division vice president, had left the company at one point to join a start-up operation but had returned after a few months to his former position, allegedly against the counsel given by this senior group human resource manager to the president of the company.

Since Andy, the senior group human resource manager, had little power base left in the organization, given the demise of the Utah plant and the related standard products division, even his boss, the vice president of human resources, couldn't help improve his status. Evidently Russell had been very pleased with the support his division was receiving from Rex, the other group human resource manager. Rex was perceived as less dogmatic, more service-oriented, and more productive than Andy. Since the announcement, Andy, who typically had been intimately involved with the affairs of closing the Utah plant, had quickly faded from our view and into the background. His distaste for Rex, long considered a rival, was widely known, and this announcement made it all the more difficult for him to save face.

Meanwhile, plant employees watched with growing detachment

and amusement as political machinations unfolded in the rest of the company. Although we once had felt a stake in what happened to the remaining company, our interests lay now with the quickly declining plant work force. The bonds of coworkers had remained strong in the plant and became the main force holding operations together. This sense of community was central in helping us work through our various coping strategies, in helping to retain contacts leading to job prospects, and in maintaining some positive energy at the plant during the difficult final months of the closure.

## Implications

### Communicate What Is Relevant

Employee morale continues to be a mitigating factor in the transition stage of the downsizing process when operation areas start to shut down and employees depart. Companies should be wary about intrusive or unnecessary practices that will offend employees or provide painful reminders of the past. The renewal process can be a very tenuous one and seemingly insignificant reminders of change may erode the progress that employees have made. Since it is often difficult to predict the effects of such downsizing transformations, companies should take caution in making any physical changes at the plant without contemplating their potential impact. If employees are given advance notice of such changes with proper explanation, negative repercussions can be minimized. This includes security measures in recalling company equipment and corporate representatives attending plant communications meetings.

Recalling company property or equipment from employees need not be a painful process. If procedures have been properly established to track and audit the use of this equipment and adequate notice is given to employees, the reacquisition process should be straightforward. Allowances can be made for employee purchase of equipment that is deemed surplus or no longer useful. Most employees will be forthright in accounting for company property in their possession, especially if they are not made to feel guilty or irresponsible by overly zealous security personnel.

Plant visits by corporate management who are associated with the downsizing are uncomfortable and often unnecessary at this stage. Companies should try to minimize contact between employees at the plant and those who represent the company's decision to downsize or close the plant. Local management should bear the responsibility to keep plant employees informed of company issues that affect them. Don't burden employees with information that is no longer relevant or of interest to them. Communication meetings should continue, but should be led by someone in plant management who is skilled at communicating sensitively and who has good rapport with employees.

### Provide for Outplacement Support

The company should have set aside some funding for outplacement support for employees at the affected plant. Not all companies can provide the same array of services as the Utah plant did, but some thought should be given to prioritizing the services that can be offered. Outplacement support that will affect the most employees and address the greatest needs may be considered first as a kind of displacement triage is established. The shutdown schedule often creates a domino effect in operational areas, which may determine the order of services to be offered. Clearly all employees will benefit from some general services: reemployment skills training, such as job-hunting, interviewing, and résumé writing. An on-site, outplacement center is a definite plus but may not be necessary if arrangements can be made to provide these services through established local community resources.

The needs of displaced workers will vary, depending on the duration of the downsizing period and the imminence of the employee's departure. Through an employee survey, these needs can be identified and a plan developed that corresponds to the shutdown schedule. Such needs may include counseling for adjustment and career planning strategies. Counseling and adjustment seminars are often available through local organizations that typically are eager to provide on-site training. Tips on networking and career planning can be useful but should be weighed against what would most benefit the employees. Many employees may simply prefer time off to seek out these services on their own. As their work loads ease, these employees should be allowed to take time off to investigate job prospects, interview, attend classes, and practice their reemployment skills.

*Allow Employees to Explore New Roles*

Employees who are still seeking jobs should explore ways to match their career interests with different jobs or tasks that need to be accomplished at the plant. Such employees will tend to stay productive because they see direct benefits in learning and using new skills, and they will become more marketable in the process. Management can encourage operations to reassign employees to new areas, where they may acquire new job skills at the same time they are helping production. Shutdown crews should be planned and identified to provide opportunities for interested employees to continue their employment with the company and defer the impending separation. The shutdown crews serve an important function for both the company and selected employees. Depending upon the nature of the production processes and the future use of the plant, there will be a need to remove equipment and clean up the facility. For those who wish to further delay their reemployment or who are still job searching, this option provides additional work time and security. Special mutual consent agreements for extensions are a tool for making these arrangements.

It is difficult to find an optimal solution in attempting to match employees' and a company's timing regarding release dates. If employees are willing to stay and work longer, mutual consent letters that offer weekly to monthly extensions from the release date period can provide the needed flexibility to bridge these gaps. Management should err on the side of caution in reformulating release dates and granting extensions to cover operational needs. Yet such extensions offer another method of reconciling employee and company desires. Additional bonuses can be provided, if appropriate, depending upon the nature of the work and technical skills required.

# 11 September
## Living with Decisions

During September, the consequences of many decisions made in the plant over the previous year finally became evident, and many of us began to reflect seriously on the consequences, both personal and company-related, of these decisions. Often the consequences were hard to recognize immediately and even more difficult to predict. Instinctively, when we find ourselves in a troublesome situation as a result of a decision we have made, we first try to find a way out of the predicament. We may resort to denial—we may attempt to act as if we had never made the decision in the first place. When we are affected by a decision made by others, we usually try to make the best out of it or find ways to cope with the consequences. We may even try to influence a change in the decision or to seek redress.

### Decision Reconciliation

For three employees, the consequences of their decisions became particularly anguishing: Brian chose to leave the company early, perhaps prematurely; Jim decided to remain with the company, later to find out how unprepared he was to deal with his new role; and Grant made a significant course correction when his decision to remain with the company caused too much personal turmoil.

Brian, a manager in the fab area, was one of the first of the professional employees in the plant to leave the company when he found another job in late February. As Brian left, he said how fortunate he felt to be able to find other work in Utah that paid comparably to what he was making at the company. He knew he was forfeiting severance and bonus pay to go out early, but he felt that the peace of

118

mind of having another job to support his family far outweighed the bonus money he was giving up.

In early September, Brian made contact with the human resources department. Stopping by the plant on the pretext to discuss professional matters, he presented human resources with a letter demanding that he be given the severance and bonus pay he had forfeited when he left. The letter stated that, on learning that some of his coworkers had made arrangements to begin work at other jobs while remaining until their completion dates, Brian felt he "would have met those eligibility requirements had they existed from the beginning." He went on to say how he was unfairly penalized "simply because I was able to find a position soon after the announcement." The letter demanded that necessary arrangements be made to grant him both severance and bonus pay.

The plant human resources manager wrote to Brian, reminding him of the terms of eligibility for severance and bonus: no one who had not met the condition of staying until their completion date had received this payment. The bonus payment was intended as a retention incentive to employees, not a consolation gift. Others had passed over job opportunities to remain with the company in order to receive this bonus. Brian couldn't accept forfeiting what could have been a fairly lucrative incentive.

Jim, the design manager who had recently transferred from the plant to New Mexico, was still recovering from the change in his role that resulted from the corporate product managers desiring their own dedicated design resources. After reviewing his situation, Jim decided to attempt to negotiate with the resident product unit manger, Hans, at the New Mexico plant. Jim realized that in order to live with the consequences of his decision to stay with the company, he would need to influence a change in the way in which the group was being divided. Partially reconciled to the reality that his position would be different from what he had originally envisioned, Jim sent an e-mail to Hans with a proposal to amend the new organization:

> After licking the salt out of my wounds, I think now if we are going to organize design by product group then we should do it right. I would pitch myself as the manager for shared resources (CAD development, device modeling, mask finishing, etc.) and maintain

functional management for design with the idea of keeping the design resources working together. This might be a way that both the specific product needs and the common, shared needs can be preserved.

After Hans responded somewhat positively, Jim decided he could now accept his limited role. If he could remain on good terms with the product unit managers who would be making competing demands on him, Jim was willing to stay with the company and give it a try. He realized now, however, what Ben, his former boss, must have gone through before deciding to leave the company.

One of the design engineers, Grant, who was still working at the Utah plant, was in the process of trying to make his transfer arrangements to New Mexico. With mounting frustration, he and his wife were negotiating with their builder in New Mexico to make some changes in the house plan. With all of the recent business he had been receiving in the New Mexico area, the local builder was intransigent: "We hold all the cards now." Grant's wife, growing more and more discouraged with the situation, had been unable to find employment opportunities in New Mexico for herself. She told Grant she was not comfortable with moving there under the circumstances.

Grant's dilemma was complicated by his lack of experience in design. He had recently moved into a design engineering position at the Utah plant in a long-awaited career step that had been difficult to make before the plant closure. Knowing that it would be nearly impossible for him to find another design engineering job in Utah, Grant was torn. He was also aware his financial liability to the company if he decided not to relocate. Nevertheless, being a strong family-oriented person, Grant knew he would never really be at peace if his family had to make all the sacrifices for his decision to stay with the company. He informed Jim that he would not be able to transfer to New Mexico and asked for a sixty-day release date, acknowledging the risk of unemployment he knew full well he was taking.

## Government Funding

Plant management's decision not to accept but to appeal the federal government denial of TRA benefits finally paid off in a decision reversal. An appeal had been filed by the plant when the denial was received in May. From additional information provided by Brent and the legal department, the Department of Labor granted the appeal and issued the following statement:

All workers of [company] in Utah who became totally or partially separated from employment on or after *February 24, 1991* are eligible to apply for adjustment assistance under Section 223 of the Trade Act of 1974.

This was joyful news to many of the employees who were planning to return to school after the closure. They reacted by thanking anyone in management at the plant who they thought might have contributed to the decision reversal. Since the gloomy news of the denial of these funds in May, most had given up any hope of financial assistance. Comments from some of these employees included "I had pretty much given up on it back in May, but this news gives me new hope and excitement for the future." "This is my ace in the hole and really makes my day!" "This is such good news! I am really jazzed!"

Local press coverage included columns in the business section of the newspaper:

FEDERAL FUNDS TO CUSHION BLOW FOR DISPLACED WORKERS

Some 970 workers, who face losing their jobs when a semiconductor manufacturer closes down later this year, are eligible for federal job-assistance funds. The money will allow employees to continue their education and get on-the-job training in other professions. "I'm ecstatic," said one worker when asked about the federal help. "People probably heard my head thump the ceiling when the message came out." "This is a chance in a lifetime. It's like a big weight lifted off my shoulders," said another worker. One employee who has been attending night school, plans to use the money to get a degree in computer science at BYU. "I was just promoted to engineer when the plant closure was announced," she said. "I've been afraid a for-sale sign might go up in front of my house."

The SOS newsletter update for September had recently noted that it was unlikely that the plant would receive the labor certification: "Committee members are not optimistic about becoming certified since the plant must prove that its closure is due to foreign competition, and that will be difficult." In the same newsletter, the committee recognized its impending difficulty in keeping track of the employees as they filtered out of the plant. Arrangements were made through the Career Transition Center to provide forms to employees that contained information to enable the committee to form a database to use in making contacts with former employees, should a buyer for the plant be found.

Since the announcement that TRA funds would be available, there had been less interest in the company-sponsored retraining classes offered through the local community college. Unfortunately, some of the employees may have used the announcement to procrastinate in their retraining efforts, thinking that government funds would take care of all their training needs. Further, according to the instructors, the attitude of some employees attending the retraining classes had degenerated. Employees reported that they were attending the class only because their supervisor had sent them. Some of these employees evidently were not accepting the responsibility to think through the repercussions of their attitudes and behavior.

Not all companies who apply for government grants in plant closures experience such positive results. But as we learned, there is nothing risked in perseverance and everything to gain. By advocating such funding, the company was helping create options for employees and becoming a partner in the employees' future pursuits.


## Site Isolation

In September, the rest of the corporation was absorbed in the budget cycle planning process, and consequently, word came to the Utah plant that all personnel requisitions in New Mexico would be frozen indefinitely. Some of the Utah employees, anticipating new positions in the New Mexico plant, were quite discouraged by the news. Apparently the company had developed a cash flow problem and needed to take conservative financial steps. Normally the Utah plant would be in sync with this budgeting cycle. But because of the closure, no such planning was occurring in the plant, and this news came as a surprise to many. It was amazing how out of touch we had become with routine company affairs.

Many Utah employees still harbored very negative feelings toward the New Mexico plant, especially the fab employees. They viewed the other plant (which contained two fab areas) as their nemesis—taking their jobs away from them. Utah employees routinely made references to the "albuturkeys" in the New Mexico plant, and resentment spilled over into a number of production and support areas. A communications training program in the Utah plant provided employees with an opportunity to externalize their feelings toward their counterparts in New Mexico. When the New Mexico plant requested transfer of the training videotapes, Brent remembered these references and tried to have the derogatory references removed from the tapes prior to sending them. "After all," commented Brent, "enough bad will exists already."

Some of the employees transferring to New Mexico sensed that there was some hostility evident toward them from the local employees. One employee, Alan (who was selected to replace one of the engineering managers in the New Mexico plant), expressed apprehensions about the environment into which he was going. The division vice president, Russell, told him that drastic changes in the New Mexico plant culture were needed. Russell perceived the Utah plant as a "can-do, highly productive volume manufacturing facility," and he had been greatly frustrated by the lack of responsiveness and urgency in the plant's culture in New Mexico. Russell wanted to replicate the productive atmosphere that had once existed in the Utah plant, and his plan was to salt the New Mexico plant with enough Utah transferees to hopefully create a cultural change.

Since several Utah managers had been named to key positions in the New Mexico plant, some of the employees there were beginning to resent them. Alan was not only going to replace one of the local managers, but would then have that same manager report to him. Further, Russell told Alan not to tell anyone about his new position until just before he transferred. Unfortunately, the other engineering manager who would be replaced heard through a technical recruiter about what was taking place. Alan was concerned about the repercussions of this change as well as Russell's expectation that he help effect a cultural transformation in the plant. Russell believed that everything was in place for the major cultural shift at the New Mexico plant: Tim was now the manufacturing manager, Alan was to join him soon as engineering manager, and there was a newly appointed plant manager. Since he was only planning to stay with the company until he completed a few more years toward his retirement, Alan felt he had nothing more to lose, despite the tremendous pressure he would be under.

New Mexico plant employees continued to resent the invasion of Utah employees long after the transfers were completed.

## Shutdown Notification

The second operation in the plant scheduled to shut down was the assembly area. Sixty-day notices were sent out to the employees in that operation. Since this was the first large group to receive the letters (the technical services area was relatively small), a week or two lead time was planned for the administrative process of getting the letters out, signed, and returned to the main company file. With 700 employees involved, the notification process was anything but simple. Problems surfaced when the assembly managers failed to pass out the letters expeditiously to the supervisors for distribution to their employees. One assembly supervisor remarked, "I'm disgusted with those managers that sit in their offices and do nothing until the last minute. Because of their procrastination, I will have to move dates back for some employees who didn't get their letters within the sixty-day time period."

In some cases, people had to scramble to ensure that the sixty-day requirement continued to be met. Since the WARN Act had passed, this was the first time the plant had to comply with the legal notification requirement. For those on vacation or medical leave, extra time had been planned to get the letters out and returned with signatures. All completion dates had been entered into the computer with a system to track them and signal when each employee's notification issuance date was due.

## Employee Communications

In the September employee communications meeting, Brent first reported a few company statistics, then moved on to discuss local plant issues. He announced an employee sale to remove the plant's excess equipment and material for the following month. This sale was the "mother of all employee sales," the largest one ever. A plant recognition and awards ceremony was also announced for 1992 performance efforts. Rather than having the nominations selected by a corporate group, however, this time they would be selected locally within the plant. Finally, Brent warned against the increased theft that was occurring in the plant. "As happens when disaster strikes, a few looters move through the area," he said, half-joking. "Take extra precautions during this time with your personal items."

When the time came for questions and answers, several hands quickly shot up. This was one of the best attended employee meetings of late, and the questions focused on the immediate concerns many of us were feeling. Some of the questions included:

How can you guarantee that what is in the employee sale the night before will still be there the next day and not be passed on to friends or outside vendors?

Why is there a hiring freeze in the New Mexico plant? How long is it going to last?

Can we buy the cafeteria and patio furniture and silk trees in the cafeteria?
—or [laughter] the light bulbs?

What will be the eligibility requirements for TRA?

How can we apply for the TRA funding assistance?

We were all trying to sort out our options and career opportunities and the financial consequences of each of those options. No one wanted to make a decision now without understanding all the potential ramifications.

## Making Casual Commitments

In September, the fab area had great cause for celebration. Breaking all previous records, workers had achieved a unit cost of $94 a wafer. Since this was a significant milestone both for the plant and the company, the fab employees wanted to celebrate their accomplishment in spite of the closure. Remembering the challenge made by the company president on his July visit, Taylor sent him an e-mail to relay this news and to accept his offer to sponsor a plant celebration when this goal was met. Part of the motivation in notifying the president of this achievement was to let him know that despite his decision to close the plant, the people in Utah were still giving it their all. Taylor and his group had managed to do the unachievable—to maintain quality levels in the fab and decrease the cost of producing the wafer at a time when volume was heading down. Taylor had also decided to make a personal commitment to stay until the end. With the added incentive of a retention bonus, Taylor secured a personal release date for February 1993. He felt that the work and determination of his engineering group, and also of the fab operators and production crew, was something to be proud of and worthy of company recognition.

The fab management team had already planned to mark the occasion with a steak fry for all of the plant fab employees. The response from the president was a terse e-mail acknowledging the accomplishment and promising to look into a celebration. A spirited fab steak fry was held shortly afterward, but no response came from corporate on the occasion. Apparently the president had passed on the assignment to ensure that something was done to celebrate this occasion to a local human resources manager. Upon hearing that a steak fry was already planned, this manager had reported that everything had been taken care of. So in the end, the only recognition given the fab area was personal pride. This further fueled the growing cynicism that the company president didn't care to reinvest any energy into the Utah facility. Some speculated that he also did not want to have to confront evidence that the decision to close the plant may have been premature.


## Closure Justification

In a presentation to a group of executive M.B.A. students at the local university, one of the plant administrative managers was asked about the plant closure impact on the rest of the company. The question concerned whether or not the decision to close the plant had resulted in overall benefits to the company's bottom line. At that point, not much data was available to indicate that the closure decision was financially wise for the company. Only Brent had this information, having pursued the same line of questioning in staff meetings with the vice president.

According to his sources, the company found itself with a $50 million problem at the end of the previous year. The parent company wanted a permanent resolution to this red ink to ensure that the problem would not recur. Each year, the company (and the industry as a whole) had been overly optimistic on product sales projections in the fourth quarter. At the end of 1991, the parent company demanded a plan with a budget revision to take the $50 million out of the sales forecast, with corresponding changes to the spending budgets. Since it cost the company around $75 million annually to operate the Utah plant, the easy answer to the budget problem as well as the capacity problem became apparent to top management.

Other options, such as product pruning and downsizing, had become annual events in the company but had never completely resolved the problem. To senior management, only a final solution such as a plant closure seemed to provide the necessary long-term guarantee to the parent company. Furthermore, as the strategic direction favored products produced in New Mexico, the Utah plant closure would eliminate the low margin, "jelly bean" business the company had been trying to work its way out of for years. Brent believed that although other viable options could have provided the long-term assurance the parent company needed, nothing proved as secure as a plant closure.

Once this decision was made, the company wrote off the estimated $20 million administrative loss from the plant closure at the end of 1991. At that point, there was really no turning back; everything was in place to make 1992 the turnaround year for the company. Unfortunately, it would be at the expense of the employees in Utah. Now that the company was turning a monthly profit, the company staff felt vindicated in their decision. On the one hand, given such profitable returns, no one could effectively dispute that the financial consequences of the plant closure weren't favorable to the company. On the other hand, there was no careful investigation of whether the same financial benefits could have been realized with other methods, resulting in less devastating consequences to Utah employees.

## Decision Politics

After carefully reworking the Utah plant employee productivity incentive proposal, which had been previously pitched to the vice president, Brent went to corporate to make the presentation to the staff. When he saw the changes, the division vice president indicated his support for the new plan and sent Brent on to discuss it with the president. As he was headed toward the president's office, the vice president of human resources stopped him. The vice president offered to deliver the proposal personally and review it with the president, lending his own support to the plan. He promised to report to Brent before the Desire Project Operations meeting (DPO) that dealt with the plant closure.

In the DPO meeting, Brent waited for the signal from the human resources vice president that it would be okay to bring up the proposal for general review and discussion. When no such signal came, during one of the breaks, Brent caught up with the vice president in the hallway to learn what had happened. He was told to go ahead and make the presentation in the meeting, since the president would be expecting it. Brent waited until the end of the meeting, then asked if it would be a good time to review the proposal. He sensed that the president was somewhat testy about the subject when it was brought up, but he was told to go ahead anyway.

As Brent concluded the presentation, he was surprised to hear the president angrily respond, "Absolutely not! That is the wrong thing to be looking at right now!" Caught off guard by this response, Brent looked to both the division vice president and the vice president of human resources for some sign of support. The division vice president looked equally surprised by the president's reaction, but the vice president of human resources face registered no expression or emotion. Since no one seemed willing to debate or support the merits of the proposal, there was no further discussion. Brent left feeling bewildered and set up. Since two finance employees from the parent company were in the meeting, Brent wondered if the president was posturing for their sake by attempting to make a point that the company was being financially conservative. Regardless of the reasons the president and the vice president of human resources behaved as they did, Brent felt a growing sense of isolation.

Brent was later told that he could resubmit a specific plan to increase the overtime pay in the Utah plant without any incentive or productivity features. This created a paradox for Utah plant employees: the company now seemed willing to pay us more just to come to work, but not for doing *more* work. Always in the past, we had been told that corporate management did not support pay plans that showed no real return on investment; in other words, they didn't reward incremental performance. When the new overtime pay plan was approved, one manager commented, "This just reinforces to me that upper management doesn't consider how their decisions impact the people." Another manager saw irony in current company incentives:

> The only person in the Utah plant now who has any incentive to perform well is the consultant who is managing the fab, and he is not an employee. The New Mexico plant is on the bonus incentive program and therefore needs to leverage the Utah fab area to run certain products and get certain results, so they can get a better bonus payout for 1992. Why didn't anyone think about linking the completion bonuses in Utah to performance? We don't have any real reason to help them out aside from our own good will.

Our perception that the rest of the company no longer cared about us and was acting as if we were already out of the picture was reinforced. It appeared that no consideration would be made for plant morale in the time remaining. Everyone was tired of hearing "You guys already have your deal," meaning the final severance package.


Solvency Concerns

Despite the good financial news the company recently conveyed, some concern remained over current cash flow. All the finance people had been instructed to hold firm on unnecessary expenses to keep costs down (not an unusual occurrence in the fourth quarter). In the assembly area, where financial information was frequently shared, this led to some fears and rumors among operators that the company might not remain solvent. Their concerns were for the company's guarantee that employees would receive their severance and bonus payouts when they left at the end of the year. Suspecting they were not getting the whole story from the company and generally anxious that something might go wrong, these employees requested reassurance from plant management that they would indeed receive their money.

Brent and the plant controller shared more financial data to try to convince employees that they had nothing to fear. By indicating the size of the restructuring budget that had been put in place to cover plant closure expenses, they were finally able to quell concerns over company financial solvency. As the end drew near, however, both people continued to receive questions about company financial policies and procedures. Clearly, many employees were now reassessing their financial situations, trying to prepare for future contingencies. For some employees, dark suspicions that the company would find a way to avoid paying out its financial obligations to them still loomed.

Some employees asked for more leniency on training reimbursement programs. In the past, there had always been fear that if an exception were granted for one employee, it would open up the floodgates for others to come forward and ask for equal consideration. In management circles, this was referred to as the dreaded rule of creating a precedent. Usually management was loathe to grant exceptions, for the fear of having to deal with other angry employees who also wanted similar concessions. Because of the closure, however, this fear had largely disappeared. In a comment to one of the other managers, Brent mentioned how liberating it was to be able to act out of compassion and common sense toward employees' requests, rather than be constrained by the fear of potential future impact: "You become much less concerned with precedent in times like this."

## Policy and Organizational Changes

Toward the end of September, two announcements that normally would have had far-reaching impact for the Utah plant employees barely made a ripple. The first announcement concerned further organizational changes in the company and outlined a new organizational structure. The second one came as a result of a recent industry study on the reproductive health of fabrication workers.

A call from the group human resources manager in California apprised the plant management that a Fax announcing the newest companywide organization structure was on its way. This announcement from the president to all managers would further clarify the restructuring program that had been underway since the first of the year:

> Per my Organizational Update, dated July 10, 1992, we have embarked on a restructure program that will complete the integration of [company] into the [parent company] Product Division. Since that time, numerous organizational changes have been announced that describe the realignment of organizational units to effect this integration. This announcement is designed to weave all those changes together and define our final organizational restructure with which we will enter 1993.

The management team in Utah greeted the announcement less than enthusiastically, and few bothered to pass the information on to the rest of the organization. They knew that few employees cared or were interested in restructuring matters, and these managers preferred to avoid another forum for confrontation with the company.

The proposed announcement on the industry study, however, caused great concern with fab management. A news item containing preliminary findings of a study, conducted for IBM by Johns Hopkins University, indicated an increase in miscarriage rate among certain photolithography fabrication workers. Corporate management was in the process of drafting and sending a memo to all employees with this information. Fab management's concern was that no plant policy changes be taken before the Semiconductor Industry Association (SIA) study results, a broader industry epidemiological study in which the company participated. These results were due at the end of the year.

Because of corporate's initial "alarmist and knee-jerk reaction," as it was denounced by the plant safety manager, the Utah plant staff feared that an employee memo might trigger a mass exodus of operators who would want early releases to leave the fab area. The plant safety manager requested a copy of the actual study findings from corporate. After carefully reviewing the document, he felt no real cause for concern, if the announcement memo were written carefully. When he tried to influence corporate safety to rewrite their draft memo, he was told that the only reason he didn't like the memo was his feelings toward the person who had written it. At this point, Brent intervened, informing corporate that the plant would not go along with the first-draft memo dated 18 September. The plant staff drafted a second memo and sent it to corporate, reiterating the current policy of accommodating concerned operators elsewhere in the fab. The offending passage of the first draft, "We instituted a practice of allowing pregnant fab employees to work outside the fab, if suitable work could be found, and if none, a leave of absence would be granted," was changed to read, "After consultation, if it appears appropriate for an employee to change locations, we intend to place the employee elsewhere within the current work area."

The memo went out to all employees, almost three weeks later than the original draft date. A few questions arose among some of the fab operators, but nothing even close to management's concerns for mass hysteria ever materialized. The closure had caused us all to become more circumspect in decisions, particularly if personal finances were involved. No one wanted to make a rash decision now that consequently would affect their wages. In the meantime, we braced ourselves for the final quarter of plant operations.

## Implications

### Establish a Policy Review Board

Policies and procedures pertaining specifically to downsizing a plant are an important tool for addressing management and employee issues during the shutdown period. These policies should explain how decisions affecting plant employees will be made. As with any policy, these should be carefully reviewed whenever questions arise that pertain to a downsizing issue, so that justice can prevail. Contingencies will nevertheless arise, and neither employees nor management will always be entirely rational in their decisions during this highly emotional period. Especially if employees sincerely attempt to deal in good faith with the company, it is wise to have a judicial process of appeal, by which mercy and clemency can be exercised. If a policy and procedure review board is established to deliberate appeals, the company will likely be consistent in administration, and at the same time allow employees to leave feeling they have received due process, as well as compassion and caring.

### Encourage Deliberation

Some employees will make imprudent decisions, later to find that they need additional help or consideration that may go against a stipulated shutdown policy. Companies can counsel employees to carefully weigh their alternatives before making final career decisions. Management can share information and try to provide employees with data relevant to their particular job situation. Not all employees will take the time to ponder the ramifications of decisions they make. Many will jump eagerly at the first viable job option they see, later to regret their hasty actions. Employees must not hold the company responsible for the decisions they make themselves. Nothing is gained by exerting energy to find culpability. Rather than bemoaning past decisions, employees should try to reconcile their circumstances and move forward. Keeping options open and creating backup plans are fruitful strategies. Most important, employees should not expect special favors or entitlements from the company when their decisions have not shown any consideration for the company's interests. Employees need to accept accountability for decisions they make throughout this period.

### Create Expectations of Equity Only

Clearly, not all employees will leave with the same financial packages or work arrangements. Comparing notes on these topics with coworkers often leads to someone feeling disgruntled or unfairly treated. Although managers should be held responsible for equitable treatment, this doesn't mean that everyone "gets the same deal." Employees should make sure that their needs are addressed without harboring resentment over what they could have received but didn't. Commitments made to employees by their supervisors at the plant become particularly significant. Managers who are looking for ways to keep morale upbeat may make statements that employees may construe as promises. Employees feel even more betrayed at this time by such irresponsible behavior. It is better to provide encouragement to these employees through ways other than enticements.

*Weigh Compliance with New Corporate Policies*

Company policy implications will continue to affect the plant, sometimes making displaced employees feel even more beleaguered. Local management should carefully assess the need for compliance to any changes in company policy that occur during the shutdown process. Some of these changes may have some relevance to the plant, but most will not. The plant should not be subjected unnecessarily to changes by the rest of the company nor expected to deal with them as part of their shutdown responsibilities. Let those who will remain with the company carry the burden of implementation.

During this particular downsizing phase, displacement of hostility may spread throughout the company, even be directed toward displaced transferring employees from employees at other company sites. These employees may resent those relocating from the plant, feeling that their relocation package was a sweeter deal than warranted. Downsizing will continue to send far-reaching effects rippling across communities and all company site locations. Depending upon the numbers of transferring employees, it may take some time for the aftermath to subside.

Some plant downsizing notification guidelines are proscribed in legal requirements, but the way these are carried out is less straightforward. Companies should take pains to ensure that proper documentation and tracking systems are in place to both comply with the requirements and provide employees with timely information as areas begin to shut down. Often, existing human resources information systems can provide the necessary database.

Because of the devastating impact of plant downsizing on employees, families, communities, and business, it is difficult to know if a shutdown decision is ever justified. Many studies have investigated the consequences downsizing and closures have had for those affected. (Bluestone 1982; Portz 1990; Rothstein 1986; Sculnick 1987). Companies should be well informed of downsizing consequences and be prepared to deal responsibly with all the stakeholders involved, including government agencies and other company site employees.

# 12 October
# Nostalgia Already?

In October, several events in the plant evoked strong feelings of nostalgia. The average seniority of those of us remaining was close to ten years, and there were strong bonds and affiliations both with the company and among fellow employees. The plant had celebrated its twenty-fifth year anniversary the previous year, and many employees believed that a plant reunion was needed before the final closure to commemorate all those years together. In addition to the reunion, there would be a huge employee sale to enable us to buy equipment, supplies, or office furniture—memorabilia that we could take with us. Finally, October marked the beginning of the sixty-day period for almost all the remaining employees; close to six hundred completion date letters went out.

The plant staff also faced a number of special circumstances pertaining to requested policy and procedure exceptions. In each case, management knew that the decisions they made would affect how employees felt about the way the company had treated them. But it also provided an opportunity to enhance the good will between employees and the company. At this point, there was strong motivation to ensure the remaining closure period would ultimately reflect favorably on the company and the people who managed the closure process.

## Notification Letters

When we finally received our own personal sixty-day notice letters, they seemed final and formal. It forced us all to stop for a minute, look back over all the time we had spent with the company, and wonder if it was all worthwhile. The letters all had the same format:

Your individual separation date has been determined and in accordance with the Workers Adjustment and Retraining Notification
Act, this letter is to advise that you will be permanently separated
from [company] on *(date)*.

Until then, there always seemed plenty of time left, but the clock
was now finally winding down. We were struck with the realization
that there was no turning back. *This was for real.*

Taylor, who had more than fifteen years with the company, asked
if he could keep his original letter instead of signing and returning it,
as required. He wanted to frame it, to remind himself that nothing
was forever. Another employee refused to sign her notice letter before she consulted with a lawyer. Perhaps she thought there might be
a loophole big enough for litigation. Some employees still struggled
with their feelings of hostility, possibly even the desire to retaliate
against the company.

Most of us remaining in the plant received our completion date
letters; more than five hundred were sent out. To date, 648 employees had been notified of their last day with the company. The
head count in October was just below seven hundred. Some thirty
employees would leave that month, around a hundred in November,
and more than five hundred employees in December. The statistics
still showed about 80 percent of employees leaving for other jobs.
Undoubtedly that number would dramatically change in December,
after the mass employee exit.

The completion letters triggered some noteworthy reactions: interest in using the outplacement center increased; the number of requests for pension estimates climbed; and some employees viewed
the letter as their contract with the company ensuring them a job
until their completion date. These employees who now thought they
had a contract tested the degree of tolerance and latitude of their
supervisors. Attendance problems escalated in the fab area, and corrective action measures were taken. One supervisor sadly observed
that he might have to fire a few people before the message got
through that the expectations of employees had not changed, nor
had the disciplinary procedures. "The last thing I wanted to spend
my time doing now was warnings," he sighed.

Plant Reunion

All former plant employees were invited to a plant reunion, an event requested by many of the employees as their final wake over the plant closure. Employees could see their former coworkers one last time before everyone went their separate ways. Some employees even hoped to do a little networking with those who had found other jobs.

The reunion was held as an open house at the plant on a Saturday between 2:00 and 6:00 p.m. More than a thousand people wandered through the plant during that time. They were greeted and signed in at the lobby entrance, where each was given a pin inscribed with the dates of the plant opening and closure. A reception area in the cafeteria offered a light buffet.

Current and former employees and their families reminisced over the time they had spent at the company and laughed at some of the collages of employee photos displayed on the walls. As they chatted about their memories of working at the plant, an occasional tear dropped and was quickly wiped away; a voice quavered for a second over recollections of more halcyon days.

Some of the employees had put together a yearbook, showing the plant assembly area and the changing profile of work areas and employee dress. Humorous captions were added to poses and mug shots of some of the employees. Finally, some company memorabilia had been collected to give away at the reunion: plastic cameras, T-shirts, mugs, and hats—all with the company logo.

Those who were interested in a tour of the plant proceeded from the cafeteria down to the assembly area. Since this area was the first operational area in the plant and had changed most dramatically over the years, many curious former employees took the opportunity to view it one last time. "Can ya' believe we spent so much time here?" a female employee exclaimed.

People from all over the state attended this final salute to the plant that had furnished employees a livelihood and memories for so many years. Some employees commented that the experience felt a little like a funeral. Interestingly, one former employee said her tenure at the plant was five of the most miserable years of her life. On hearing this, Brent, who had helped to greet people as they came in, scratched his head and wondered why that individual had bothered to come back and participate in an event that evoked such negative feelings for her. Almost everyone who attended, however, felt very good about the experience and expressed thanks to those who had been responsible for organizing it. For most people, nostalgic experiences such as these brought back sentimental feelings; some employees were able to justify to themselves that their time at the company was well spent.

## Employee Sales

A memo had recently come from the plant staff announcing that employees would be allowed to purchase their own office furniture when they left. A standard price was listed for each item, including bookshelves, desks, file cabinets, tables, and chairs. This generated immediate interest, not because we necessarily needed those items, but because this was an opportunity to take a piece of our work area and memories with us when we left.

More than three hundred employees showed up at the sale, which started at 7:30 a.m. on a Saturday. People were lined up at each entrance, waiting for the signal to enter the building. Some employees were in line for more than an hour, hoping to get first shot at the items they were interested in. The sale was held in one of the empty fab shells. One of the security managers counted down from ten and then let people run for the sale items. Surprisingly, despite the chaos that ensued, there was no contest over items, thanks to the opening of the area for employee perusal before the sale.

The other reason for little squabbling over the items was the speed with which people ripped off tags from the items. Once the tag was pulled, the employee with the tag had the right to purchase the item. Caught up in the frenzy of the moment, some employees had indiscriminately torn off tags with little idea of what they were about to purchase. Other employees were simply stunned by the low prices and wanted to take every advantage of this once-in-a-lifetime sale.

Employees who were unable to purchase items at this large sale learned of other smaller employee sales through the remainder of the year. Further, there would be giveaway items, located at the lobby entrance, which the plant finance people had accounted for as no value to the company. Items such as data books, binders, telephone cords, empty wafer cassettes, and manuals had been cleaned out of areas and declared waste material. Almost every day the employees came through the lobby entrance, they found new opportunities to carry away some small company memento. Needless to add, these items were snapped up quickly and cleared out almost before the end of each day.

Shirley had been enthusiastic about helping out with and participating in both the plant reunion and large employee sale. She seemed to thrive on finding ways to be useful and occupied with events that benefited the employees. She laughed about the mass of bodies charging through the doors at the employee sale, as she was helping direct traffic: "It felt like I was going to be swept away somewhere where no one would ever find me again." Shirley was also the focal person at the Utah plant in helping to administer employee relocation offers and transfers to the New Mexico plant. She took pains to spend time with each employee who was entertaining an offer and became almost indispensable in keeping the relocation process operating smoothly. When a relocation survey was administered by corporate asking how the employees viewed the support they were receiving, Shirley was shocked to read some of the bitter and caustic feelings of a few of the transferred employees. Trying not to take the feedback personally, she joked, "I guess you just can't please everyone. Next time I go through this, I'll be better!"

## Transferring Products

The plant received word that a contract had been negotiated with a small fabrication foundry located in Arizona, which would produce the old small logic parts from the Utah plant that would not be transferred to the New Mexico plant. These parts had been the bread-and-butter business for the plant and company for many years. For some employees who had worked closely with these products, the news that the products would no longer be produced by the company triggered nostalgia. Some of the employees still felt strong attachment to these old products and wondered how they could obtain some of these parts with the company's logo still on them. The official memo announcing the contract contained the following information:

Our new agreement with [foundry] is a result of the company's worldwide effort over many months to solicit interest in the Utah product line assets. It also concludes our plan to sell the tooling, product inventories, and license intellectual property rights for these products to the most qualified continued product manufacturer for our customers with the best overall financial return to [company] and [parent company]. The transfer of our product line assets will occur only after we have completed the manufacture of products for our customers last time buy orders or contracts that [company] must fulfill as part of the final build schedules in Utah.

Many customers who sought these parts were skeptical of the success of a product transfer to a foundry operation where quality and process viability could be compromised. They preferred to try to get their parts produced at the Utah plant before the closure. Unfortunately, the window of opportunity for the products to start through the fab and be completed before the operation closed down was quickly narrowing. Also, the Utah fab employees had no real incentives to increase their work volume when their release dates remained the same.

The foundry operation in Arizona had been determinedly recruiting Taylor to join them. They realized the pivotal role he could play in ensuring a smoother transfer of products and process to that facility. It was also in both companies' best interest to see this transfer process occur successfully. Since Taylor had been willing to stay at the plant through February 1994, several managers at corporate pulled strings to ensure that everything could happen to encourage Taylor to join the foundry firm. Although he didn't flaunt his offer, Taylor was clearly pleased with the terms he was able to work out and that he and his family could accept the offer to go to Arizona in February.

## Buried Treasures

Departments were engaged in the task of using up their last supplies of office goods, production materials, and equipment parts. Storage areas were being cleaned out and materials sorted for either the employee sale or for disposal. In the process of cleaning out closets and file drawers, one of the department secretaries came across a box of old photos from the SigScene, a plant newsletter produced in the 1980s, photos of current and former employees at company-sponsored events, dating back to the 1960s when the plant first opened.

As the box was passed around for other intrigued administrative employees to view, there were shouts of laughter and cries of delight as old familiar faces were pointed out and recognized. This cache of photos covered long-since forgotten company recognition parties, open houses, Christmas parties, and sports events. Arrangements were made to give some of the photos to employees still with the company. Consequently, some employees received an old photo of themselves that stirred a vivid recollection of past moments in their tenure with the company.

## Exceptions to Policy

During October, the plant managers had to confront some individual cases that required consideration of exception to policy. In each case, the individual's circumstance was reviewed carefully to determine the legitimacy of granting an exception. At the same time, the managers realized that any extraordinary or unusual plant decisions would quickly be broadcast and become general knowledge. As a result, the staff became more aware of how their decisions would affect employee morale. In a shift to relax precedent, the plant managers tried to make decisions that would allow people to leave with good feelings about how the company had treated them. Two cases in point follow.

Three female operators in the assembly area were preparing to go out on medical leave. Each was concerned, however, that according to the plant closure policy, if they were not able to return to work on their completion date, they would forfeit their completion bonus. All three had spoken with the plant nurse, who lobbied on their behalf for the managers to grant them an exception, owing to the nature of their illnesses. All three were long-term employees (twelve or more years) and had a life threatening condition: one of the employees had Parkinson's disease and would be going on long-term disability; one required regular dialysis treatment; and one would be entering the hospital for brain surgery. In each case, the medical leave was unavoidable.

When the management staff reviewed the issue, one manager quickly offered a perfunctory "no," reiterating the closure policy. The manager of health services retorted that the plant had more to lose by denying the completion bonus to these three employees than by being consistent with policy. Fearing potential repercussions of a class action suit, the first manager contended that the plant management should not depart from its stated course to deny these exceptions. Another of the managers from human resources then spoke up: "We need to be more concerned about doing the right thing than doing things the right way at this point. We have our collective conscience to consider. I think if other employees found out about these exceptions, they would feel that the company was doing the right thing as well."

The decision was made to grant the three employees an exception to policy and allow them to go out on medical leave without returning to work; they would still receive their competition bonuses. Ultimately, the good will this action generated from the three employees benefited the group as a whole. No employee protested the action as unfair or discriminatory.

## Retention Bonus

At the time of the closure announcement in January, the plant staff had designated certain employees as eligible for an additional retention bonus if they stayed until their release dates. The intent of this compensation program was to identify those employees whom the company was at high risk of losing to other jobs and who were also functioning in critical job positions. Only so many designations were allowed; the criteria were stringent and required that the employee perform a role deemed crucial to a smooth plant closure.

The retention bonus eligibility issue surfaced when an employee in finance discovered, through a coworker in payroll who had access to the list, that her name was not on the list. The employee, Carla, felt that her role in tracking plant assets through the first quarter of 1993 entitled her to receive this additional compensation. What further galled her was her discovery that one of her coworkers in finance, who had less time with the company, was on the list to receive a retention bonus. Carla marched indignatly into her supervisor's office to confront him with her findings.

Caught by surprise, the supervisor was unprepared to answer all Carla's questions. Since Carla's supervisor was also fairly new to the plant and had not been involved in the retention bonus designation process, he asked for some time to look into the situation. Now emotional, Carla left the plant to calm down before discussing the matter further. As she sat at home stewing over what she saw as an inequity, she decided to press her case further. Charging the plant management with discrimination, Carla called Brent to tell him that she was not planning to return to work until she had received a satisfactory response on her grievance. She claimed this to be the worst thing that had ever happened to her during her professional career and took it as a personal insult that she was excluded from retention bonus consideration.

Brent explained to Carla that nothing could or would be done until she returned to work. He promised to follow up on the issue when she returned and affirmed that the company would not respond to threats. Carla pulled herself together and returned to the plant. Later that day, Brent and the supervisor met with her to review the situation. Brent tried to explain the rationale behind the retention bonus. He confirmed that she was indeed a valuable employee who performed a vital function; her performance was not at issue. He pointed out that when the closure announcement was made, she had indicated her interest in remaining until the end and had expressed no desire to leave the plant before her release date in March 1993. Given this information, albeit her function could have made her a candidate, management had not included her on the list for a retention bonus, since the purpose of the bonus was to induce retention.

Carla accepted this information reluctantly, but reiterated her complaint that her coworker—whom she considered less hard-working than herself—also should not have been eligible. Again, Brent explained that when the judgment was made on who seemed most likely to leave the company, this particular employee was deemed a high risk. Carla then requested that both Brent and the supervisor meet with the rest of her department to explain this program to them. She had apparently told them all about her personal feelings and made them aware of the retention list, which was considered confidential information. The finance department that Carla supervised already considered themselves the poor step-children of the plant when it came to company fringe benefits. In their positions, they were very familiar with the spending habits of other departments and knew instantly when special privileges were granted. Consequently, they had become more and more dissatisfied with the "special treatment" they saw around them but weren't able to receive themselves. Furthermore, Carla had taken upon herself the role of plant capital asset protector. In a few instances, she had alienated both Brent and her own supervisor by going around them to protest to corporate about plant decisions she felt were unwise disposal of capital assets. In one case, she had sent an e-mail to the company vice president of finance complaining about the "pilferage" she perceived was taking place in the plant. As a result of her actions and what others saw as her "blue collar mentality," Carla garnered little sympathy from either her supervisor or Brent over her current dilemma.

Nevertheless, Brent felt obligated to revisit the retention bonus decision and review whether Carla's exclusion was still appropriate. Since her job function had become more critical over time and there was some concern about her tendency to become "walking wounded" in the plant if she remained unhappy about her situation, Brent considered other options. He felt that although Carla did not meet the criteria for a retention bonus, there might be a way to provide an incentive for her to stay and maintain her performance level—to help her move past her feelings of having been mistreated. The final resolution attached a confidentiality clause. Carla accepted the conditions presented to her, feeling that her concerns had been justly dealt with.


Employee Communications

In the October employee communication meeting, Brent announced a major milestone for the company. As a result of improved sales volume, the company was now $1.4 million profitable for the year overall; $4 million was profit just from September. Later, one of the finance people would comment that this was just "funny money," the result of the percentage drop in employee benefits alone. Brent commented that the company was doing well for two reasons: the huge amount of high-priced customer last-time buys (in some cases two- to three-year orders were placed), and the general strength of the market. Employees greeted the news with understandable coolness.

A group of employees then presented an award to Brent in recognition for his efforts in reversing the Department of Labor's decision on TRA funds. An employee spokesperson presented him a pair of binoculars and thanked him for his "vision and focus" in getting the TRA monies approved for the plant. Brent, visibly touched by this gesture, became speechless for a moment as he recovered from the surprise. He voiced his appreciation and then made one last announcement about temporary employees:

> Those of you who are Kelly temporaries had asked that we look into the possibility of converting you over to full-time for a short period to allow you eligibility for the TRA training benefits. We have consulted with our legal advisor and after careful consideration, we have decided not to do this. We feel that it compromises our integrity with the government agencies and the taxpayers, and gives rise to too many legal ramifications in some other areas.

Although the approximately fifty plant temporary operators showed disappointment at the news, many of them had apparently anticipated this outcome. A few of them were obviously out to seize any opportunity to capitalize on plant closure benefits.

## Administrative Considerations

As certain departments begin to slow down due to the nature of their work, other areas in the plant were inundated. The uneven flow of work caused some consternation among the employees. In the human resources department, activity had picked up, especially in the benefits area. Because employees were all asking for pension information as their completion dates became imminent, the plant staff requested that all estimates be completed over the next two weeks. The benefits supervisor, feeling embattled, resisted having other employees help with the estimates. She was doing all of them herself because she knew that all pension estimates must be done manually and she feared that the involvement of others would introduce errors. She spent personal time trying to do the approximately six hundred pension estimates. Finally, realizing the futility of trying to do the entire task by herself, she enlisted support from the rest of the department and asked the corporate benefits people to come in November to assist before the mass exit processing occurred.

The assembly area was slowing down and running out of work for employees. In a staff meeting, the assembly management team discussed paying people through their completion dates and letting them go out earlier. Since they had extended employees' completion dates originally because of a larger forecasted schedule, they felt some obligation to compensate their people through the closure period. When the fab management heard about this possible strategy of pay for no work, they reacted strongly: "If they pay their people and send them home, we will have a mass uprising from fab employees." The issue was taken to plant management for discussion and resolution. Short of reaching a hard closure on the matter, the managers decided that every effort should be made to find work for people to do rather than send them home with pay. This issue would later pose one of the more significant employee morale problems of the plant closure. For now, the matter was dropped, in hopes that a low-key approach, letting each area manage its work assignments, would resolve the problem.

## Tension and Anxiety

Now that the end was quickly approaching and the notice period had arrived, we found ourselves a little on edge. The general anxiety had returned, bringing with it the fear that we would be left without jobs and means to provide for ourselves. Most of us had managed until now to suppress our worries about the closure and reemployment process. But the apprehensions had come back with a vengeance, along with anxiety dreams at night. As we struggled to cope with the fear of the unknown, tensions among coworkers were more apparent.

Jesse spoke of his frustration at being right on the verge of closing on a job offer, yet still awaiting a final confirmation. He expressed the helplessness he felt, which he didn't want to convey to his prospective employer: "I've been patient for almost ten months now, and I have a sense of urgency to get this offer. I want to scream and shout to this employer, *Don't you know I've been waiting long enough? Make the offer now!*"

Some of the employees in the fab were having difficulty with their supervisors and felt that supervisors were not demonstrating enough empathy toward them and the stress they were experiencing. One particular team on graveyard began hounding the manager about this supervisor's "heavy-handed" behavior. The team claimed that the supervisor, Steve, was too insensitive and showed no appreciation for their efforts. Suddenly, one morning there appeared an anonymous memo under the doors of the two fab managers and the plant manager:

We are fast approaching the end of our jobs at Signetics, yet people continue to do their work with hardly a ripple. Numbers are up and scraps have been relatively few considering our current situation. For some reason the TAs [supervisors] feel like the time has come to put the pressure on. They have started dogging their people around the fab, counting the time cards to the very second, taking control and dictating on issues that normally are handled by the team. Some TA's have prevented portions of their team from attending team parties because they had "too much work." Some TA's hover over their people watching their every move in the hopes of catching them doing something wrong. Please tell them to back off! We work better and are less likely to develop attitude problems if we are treated decent. *At this point we need people who know how to build morale, not people who only know how to crack the whip!*

On reading the memo, both fab managers suspected that the same graveyard team had been responsible for the memo. They chose not to respond to the anonymous letter, claiming that if the sentiment reflected in the memo was representative, they would undoubtedly hear it from other employees. Instead, there was a general appeal to all fab employees and management to be more tolerant of each other. "After all," commented one of the managers, "who isn't stressed out by now and acting defensively?"

## Recognition Celebrations

Since the assembly operation was the next area to shut down, the group decided to hold their last big recognition celebration on Halloween. Employees in the assembly area had the most seniority in the plant and therefore had more at stake with the plant closing. These employees were nevertheless determined to make their last weeks at the company both memorable and fun. They decided to hold a costume party; teams would compete in dressing up their supervisors most outrageously. With shouts of encouragement and raucous laughter, the teams led their decorated supervisors through the conference room, where all the assembly employees were packed to witness this special occasion. Each costume seemed more bizarre than the last. The supervisors appeared to take it all in stride, parading through the room, looking the likes of Elvis, the Ghost of the company's Past, a robot from outer space, Lady Godiva on a saw horse, a bumblebee, and a car-crash victim. When the shouts and laughter died down, the costume awards were presented and the official recognition ceremony began.

One of the managers then announced that a roast of the company president had already occurred the night before. He joked about the many corporate requests to start "the last lot" through the assembly area. One product request was going through production that very day on the STR (prototype) line, a "hot" product that was needed by January 1994. The manager chuckled that this would be perfect timing, since by that time corporate people could be sent up to train on that line without operators or any production support resources. As the beacon awards (the outstanding individual quality award) were handed out, a gold badge and $1,000 were given each honoree. "If you hurry, you might still be able to get in on the special deal and trade your gold badge and $1,000 in for some Utah plant company stock that will be good until you 'retire' or 2,020, whichever date comes first," the manager teased. After the ceremony, the entire group of more than one hundred employees met at a local restaurant to have their "last supper" together before individuals started leaving.

Years ago in more robust times, the company had given away gifts to the employees at the holiday season—a box of candy, a gift certificate, or a turkey at Thanksgiving time. When a chunk of money was discovered in the employee recreation fund, the plant staff discussed the notion of a holiday season giveaway. Since this fund was created for the express use of the employees, no one felt comfortable simply turning the money back to the company. Furthermore, as the holiday season approached, the opportunity to do something nice for remaining employees appealed to the staff. The decision was to provide $20 gift certificates to all the remaining employees and to use the rest of the money to sponsor recognition events throughout the year.

## Company Memorabilia

We received an announcement from the company president regarding the company's identity shift to the parent company name. An e-mail message was sent to all employees, explaining the sequence of events that would signal this identity shift.

> This message is to update you on the status of the program to shift our identity from [company] to [parent company]. Our official shift date is January 1, 1993, although we will be changing signs and stationery and some merchandising materials during the fourth quarter of 1992.

The text also itemized all the materials that would no longer carry the company's old name, including business cards, stationery, forms and documents, fax messages, and company memorabilia. "If you want to hang on to the oldies for sentimental reasons, your scrapbook is the place for them!" the president emphasized. Corporate management was unaware of the special significance this message would carry in the Utah plant, and there was no mention of the plant being excluded from these events. When a call came from corporate asking if the plant wanted to participate in the identity shift events and associated hoopla, the plant staff emphatically declined. Not only would the plant closure mark the first of its kind with the company, it would now also signify the closing of an era for the company in its transformation and shedding of the old skin. The irony of the timing of this event was not lost on us.

## Implications

### *Plan Events for the Plant Community*

Most employees, especially those with seniority at the affected plant, will wax nostalgic as they see the plant community begin to break down. At the Utah plant, the average tenure was close to a decade, and this provided powerful motivation for departure ceremonies. Some employees had been at the plant since its inception over twenty-five years ago. Departure ceremonies and rituals provide a meaningful way for plant employees to reconcile their past and present status with the company. To some degree, we all need to be able to look back at the past and feel that our activities were successful and our time well spent.

Ceremonies that celebrate employee wins and recognize performance create meaningful ways for employees to remain upbeat and productive. Employees need to feel appreciated and valued throughout this time but particularly as they prepare to leave. The resources necessary to sponsor these celebrations are minimal relative to the significant impact they can have. Employees can help ease the financial concerns that weigh against sponsoring such events by volunteering their time and offering low-cost options to management. These events can be held during off-hours, thereby avoiding both interference to operations and obligation for those who may choose not to participate. Work areas may want to plan regular get-togethers as something coworkers can look forward to each week or month— fun and memorable milestones in the otherwise relentless, inevitable progress of reductions-in-force.

Plant reunions may not be appropriate for all companies. If approved, however, they should be grassroots efforts orchestrated by employees, not management. Depending upon the level of community spirit at the plant, a reunion can be somewhat cathartic for departing employees. These events do take considerable organization and require some funding support from the company. If employees express a desire for such a reunion, companies should willingly grant the approval and resources necessary.

As we discovered, employee sales can also absorb considerable time and energy from those involved. Arrangements for inventory identification and tracking, price determination, equal access of items to employees, and final dispensation can require much planning and preparation. Employees, nevertheless, often are willing and eager to help out with these arrangements. The sales are mutually beneficial for employees (great prices for desired items) and the company (elimination of unwanted assets) and can generate good will if handled properly. Management should be careful to provide advance notice of the sales to ensure that each plant employee has a chance to participate.

Managers can help to promote this type of event and encourage employees to become involved. Assigning teams who are now mostly idle to help generate and implement such ideas is an alternative to sending home people who may prefer to stay and help out at work. By providing opportunities for employees to reflect positively on their experiences with the company, company policymakers can help displaced employees move forward into employment prospects with greater equanimity. Employees will need some time to grieve over the loss of friendships and community, which for some may have become a central support system in their lives. Through events like reunions, auctions or sales, and even roasts, employees can better come to terms with the shutdown. These events can also help employees generate positive energy to face their departure. Ultimately the loss of community has significant impact on all displaced workers. The company can help employees savor this precious asset a little longer by encouraging and sponsoring such ceremonies.

*Consider Late Exceptions to Policy*

Clearly, granting exceptions to policy can be one of the most difficult management issues to resolve. Whenever an exception is granted, there will always be those who feel exceptions should also be made for them. But if no provision exists for considering exceptions, displaced employees may rally together to take action against the company for insensitive treatment. Such issues are complex and require careful attention throughout the downsizing period.

Not all employees who are offered retention bonuses will elect to stay until the required time. This may precipitate a need to reassess eligibility and consider other employees for the bonus. We discovered that retention bonuses should be discrete compensation items and not part of the general severance packages. These bonuses are typically used as an incentive for key technical employees who may have reason to leave the company before their release period (see Appendix 3). Normally these bonuses are planned and offered at the beginning of the closure process, shortly after the announcement. Unfortunately, unless the specific financial agreements are kept confidential, they can be a source of animosity between employees who feel they are deserving and the company. It is advisable for management to be clear about the existence of these bonuses and the criteria for awarding them, without disclosing the identity of recipients.

### Continue Communicating

Plant communications will continue to become more difficult when operations are winding down and some employees may feel no inhibition in expressing themselves. Employee communication meetings should continue, however, and provide a forum where these feelings can be aired. Despite the discomfort management may feel in handling these meetings, employees need this forum to vent frustrations which may otherwise find more destructive outlets.

### Fulfill Legal Notification Requirements

Final notification letters must be provided to all employees who will be permanently separated from a company. These letters should contain certain specific information, including the closure date, the individual employee's last day of work, and the legal requirement for appropriate notification time (see Appendix). No matter how these letters are worded, they tend to have a sobering effect on employees. Nevertheless, the blow is somewhat softened if the letter contains more than the necessary legal protocol. By adding a personal word of gratitude for the contributions plant employees have made, management can help employees to regard their final days at the plant with a little more pride. Even the process of distributing the letters can make a difference if managers try to carry this out with a human touch.

# 13 November
## Down to the Wire

In a marathon—particularly for runners who have never participated in one before—the initial burst of excitement and energy they feel about the race quickly dissipates as the reality of the length and arduousness of running becomes apparent. At first, runners watch their competition to pace themselves and sense how many other runners are also struggling. But eventually, as the end approaches and the finish line is in sight, a runner's only concern is to finish the race. Winning or even doing well becomes secondary to the goal of completing the race. As the end draws near, the runner becomes obsessed to find the strength to endure and finish the race as quickly as possible.

Each of these emotions was familiar to those of us who had stayed at the plant until November. The metaphor of a marathon seemed very fitting. As we got down to the wire—the closure—many of us were weary, weary of all the activities needed to close departments and finish off tasks, of expending energy on short-term projects, of trying to make each day challenging enough to face coming to work. Even the recognition activities and parties in the plant were becoming tiresome. Most of us were counting down our remaining days and paychecks to determine what time and energy we would need to spend to complete the task.

### Compensation Issues

The fab graveyard operators, running out of work, sat idle. Fab managers were trying to find projects for them both inside and outside the fab. The workload was obviously getting progressively unbalanced. Those who were busy resented those who were not. There was suspicion that the recent errors in the fab may have been partly due to the lack of focus and concentration caused by the idle operators bothering others who had work to do. People who had run out of work were requesting to go out early, rather than do make-work projects that only reminded them of their idleness and impending unemployment. Managers were trying to be creative by loaning out employees to shift the burden more equitably. Training classes were scheduled on company time to help fill the remaining hours.

Workers in one production area that would work busily to the very end, the test area, complained about what they termed "discriminatory pay practices" that other areas were exercising. Since not every idle operator had been given other work to do, some of the supervisors in assembly and fab were sending their people home on paid time. A few of the test operators were incensed when they learned of this, since they were unable to participate in this perceived benefit. They demanded to know why they couldn't be granted this same benefit instead of being "penalized" for working in the last area to shut down. One employee, Sally, was relentless in her criticism of the company and how she had been mistreated over the years.

> This company has always been discriminatory against women and operators. I don't see why we should suffer while others get all of this extra pay for no work. We're always the ones who get left out. I'm sick of the way I get treated around here and if they try and ask me to stay longer (a possibility discussed by her supervisor), my response will be, "Why should I?"

When Brent learned of this impending morale problem, he decided that some general plant guidelines were needed to deal with this issue of pay for no work. A memo was routed to all supervisors and managers:

> As the various production areas slow down and discontinue operations, some employees will have time available for a variety of projects that need to be completed as part of the plant closure. Anytime employees have completed their operating job assignment and have time available, follow these guidelines in sequential order:

1. Coordinate within operating areas to move people to available work within other operations.
2. Utilize employees to maintain housekeeping and operating standards and prepare the operating area for closure.
3. Contact the project coordinators for your operating area for project work assignments. These coordinators will match project needs with available resources.
4. Allow people to review training materials or do retraining activities.
5. Allow people to use the Career Transition Center.
6. As a last resort, send people home. Since we are in the sixty-day notice period, any involuntary time off must be paid. Be sure that any time off is equitably distributed among team members.

This memo assuaged the concerns of these employees for the moment. But as soon as this issue seemed to be resolved, another quickly surfaced. When fab employees heard about the assembly area's recent recognition awards, they became concerned about the selection process for beacon award winners and the award's potential for divisiveness. A group of fab operators met with Brent to complain about the pending fab recognition event. The potential damage of selective awards, they contended, would, "tear the fab apart." These same employees suggested that the total award value ($10,000) might be divided equally among all the fab employees.

Brent was incredulous. Did they really think that the ten $1,000 awards were worth trading for a lousy $14 per employee? He reminded these employees that some workers had put forth exceptional effort throughout the year and deserved substantial recognition. He asked them, "Do you really begrudge these people that money if they truly deserve it?" Somewhat chastened, these employees conceded that certain people had worked hard compared to others who barely showed up for work each day. Brent convinced these employees that the rest of the plant viewed the awards as positive; the ceremony should proceed as planned. From employee feedback, however, fab management decided not to hold a big fab meeting with all employees, as assembly had done, but rather pass out the awards in a small, informal gathering in one of the fab manager's offices. As a result of this low-key approach, few problems emerged.

Each Friday during the mass exit interviews with departing operators, some employees became quite emotional about leaving the plant and their friends. One employee wore dark glasses to the exit meeting, so the difficulty of her departure would not be so obvious. Employees who had purchased their office equipment clogged the hallways on Fridays as they wheeled out desks and file cabinets. Employees wandered the hallways, saying their last goodbyes, looking for friends to visit with. Also on Fridays, as part of the dispersal of recreation fund money, donuts and punch were made available to employees in the cafeteria. One fab employee was particularly incensed when her supervisor chastened her for not returning to her work after over a one-hour break for free snacks in the cafeteria. "How can he expect us to work a normal routine anymore?" she demanded.

## Job Fairs

To step up outplacement support, a job fair sponsored by the outplacement center was held in early November; about ten local employers participated. A luncheon in the cafeteria enticed employees to pass by the recruiting booths. Large groups of employees attended throughout the afternoon, depositing their résumés and applications with selected companies that were represented. The plant staff had run an advertisement in all the local papers the week before to attract the attention of Utah employers and to communicate that employees would now be available for other work. The ad also recognized those of us who had stuck with the company to the end.

MANY THANKS!! TO ALL SIGNETICS EMPLOYEES FOR:
Record Setting Quality Results and
World-Class Manufacturing Performance
ATTENTION: PROSPECTIVE EMPLOYERS

Signetics operations in Utah will close on 15 December 1992. As a result, we have established a formal Career Transition Center to help in the outplacement of our outstanding workforce. Signetics employees have diverse skills and seek a full range of opportunities from entry to senior level positions. . . . (listing of job types).

Should you have need for quality personnel experienced in a team-oriented environment, please contact our Career Transition Center.

Evidently, many job leads were forwarded to the outplacement center. Several employees expressed appreciation for the gesture. Some outside applicants who, not having closely scrutinized the text of the ad, also sent their résumés to the center, thinking that actual jobs would be offered.

## Public Relations

Now that the first of the mass exits had begun, local news reporters called the plant for details. Brent received requests from several who wanted to interview departing employees. One local reporter had kept a tickler file on the plant closure and cited the very week the first operation (assembly) would begin shutting down. The fact that the day happened to be Friday the thirteenth added drama to the reported event:

SUN SETTING ON PLANT AS FRIDAY THE 13TH DAWNS

Friday the 13th marked the beginning of the end for the Signetics integrated-circuit manufacturing plant that will soon cease to be the area's fourth-largest employer. One of the workers who lost her job Friday, a 10-year employee of the plant described the situation as sad. "The worst part is leaving the people—we've been one great big family," she said. Another employee described the situation as "scary." "The hard part was sending out résumés and getting nothing back," he said, adding that if he moved away from Utah, he could get a job right away. However, he has just purchased a home. "I never realized how useless my degree was until this happened." He plans to continue his education and perhaps combine another subject with his current degree.

At its peak, the plant employed 2,000 people. So far, 100 have been transferred to other jobs with the company out of state and another 100 have left voluntarily. The plant manager said 80% of those leaving have found jobs on their own.

A local evening television news report picked up the story as it hit the wire service, mentioning that "pink slips" were being handed out. We employees who heard the story wondered why "pink slips" was used, since such slips were no longer a feature of a layoff. The term created a more dramatic image of employees losing their jobs.

The forty or so people from assembly (mostly women) who were leaving that week seemed relatively calm and accepting of the exit process. They were somewhat taken aback by all of the attention their leaving had drawn in the community. The only unique aspect to their departure was that they were the first large group of employees to be reduced in force. During their exit, several asked if they might keep their company badges as a memento. Since about half of them were not planning to move to another job, this would be their last experience in the job market. As the group exit meeting closed, one of the employees stood up and shouted, "Goodbye everyone!" This triggered a round of applause and handshakes. Each filed out of the meeting room, saying their final farewells to team members and friends who in most cases would part ways for good.

Partly because of all the press coverage, the plant had been inundated with calls from "financial consultants" who wanted to solicit investments from the money that would become available from employee pension and 401K rollovers. Most of them were lobbying to do consulting with employees on site in group meetings sponsored by the company. The plant managers were was reluctant, however, to sponsor any of these on-site meetings. They feared that sanctioning some would require doing it for all, and they wanted to avoid the appearance of endorsing a particular financial institution. Rather than hold these meetings on-site, the plant elected to post all advertisements and information on company bulletin boards.

One particular financial consultant, a former employee at the plant, decided to be more aggressive. He showed up at the lobby one day on the pretense of having an appointment with one of the employees. Using the lobby telephone, he called all the employees he used to know until he found one willing to come out and sign him into the plant. He wandered from office to office, soliciting employee interest in his financial services. Finally one employee, disturbed by the blatant solicitation, alerted security to the situation. Security tracked down the consultant, escorted him to the door, and warned him to never return.

Some employees were now easy marks for this kind of solicitation. Most of us were eager for specific information on the amount and timing of our pension and 401K payouts. There were meetings to provide us this information. Corporate benefit representatives showed up a few days in advance to finish off all pension estimates that still needed to be calculated. In mass meetings of up to sixty employees, people from the local unemployment office also provided information on services available to displaced workers—everything from unemployment benefits to state social services support agencies. A packet handed out to each employee detailed the following topics: understanding typical reactions to job loss, planning a budget, unemployment insurance, job services, dislocated worker letter, mortgage information, utility assistance, counseling services, and labor market and job-search information (see Appendix 2).

With 635 employees still remaining at the plant, multiple information meetings were scheduled to help employees make the transition out of their jobs. The meetings lasted around two and a half hours and were filled with useful suggestions on how to manage the transition. Although some employees remained bitter to the end, most questions in the meetings were upbeat and the climate positive.

## Employee Communications

The final plant employee communication meeting took place in mid-November. On his last visit through the plant before the closure, the division vice president came to deliver a parting message. First, Brent reviewed some company statistics and a few local plant items.

As of the end of October, the company was reporting a $6 million profit. Brent pointed out that the plant closure was indeed responsible for some of this, especially in the return on assets numbers. Many employees reacted to this comment with stony silence and sideways glances at coworkers to register their skepticism. Most plant employees remained convinced that the closure was the biggest possible mistake the company could have made; few believed that it could do anything but negatively affect company operations. Brent reported another job fair in January, coincident with another printing of the advertisement announcing the closure to prospective local employers. Then, Brent turned the remaining time over to the vice president for his message.

The vice president was greeted with considerable coughing and murmuring from the audience. His presence was not welcome at the Utah plant. Undaunted, he cleared his throat a few times to get attention and proceeded with his prepared text. Praising the plant performance and the new standards that had been set despite the stressful times, he thanked us all for our continued dedication and hard work. Citing one of the largest customer's initial concerns about the plant closure, he added that this customer now wanted to pass on thanks to all the Utah employees for the great job we had done. He read a letter of appreciation to employees from the Programmable Logic Devices (PLD) product group. It elicited snickers from the audience. Finally, he came to his closing statement: "I salute you for taking your performance to new levels this year, despite the difficulties of the year." Realizing that his words were having little effect on the hostile group, the vice president quickly sat down.

Sensing everyone's awkwardness, Brent stood up to close the meeting. He cited positive feedback from some local employers who had hired plant employees; Brent told how impressed many of them were with the plant employees they had hired. He referred to his comments in the April employee communication meeting on how the closure would reflect on each of us as employees. Suggesting that the closure had some positive aspects, he stated that each employee would benefit from having participated in this painful yet "successful" event. From the faces in the audience, it was clear that Brent's words struck a chord with us. Brent reminded us that we could still take pride in our accomplishments at the plant. That felt good.

Ironically, just as we were preparing to wind down the final closure activities, an edition of *Time* magazine carried a feature story on the rebound of the semiconductor industry, "Chips Ahoy!"

Not too long ago, the U.S. semiconductor industry faced extinction. American manufacturers were devastated by foreign competition during the past decade. The semiconductor industry lost more than $4 billion and 25,000 jobs between 1983 and 1989. Dozens of firms abandoned the business. Written off by many experts, the semiconductor industry seemed destined for the same fate as steel, autos and televisions.

Like a high-tech phoenix, the U.S. semiconductor industry appears to be rising again. Rejuvenated by innovative product lines, protectionist trade policies and state-of-the-art manufacturing, chipmakers are staging a stunning comeback. The U.S. share of the market has surged to 42% this year, up from the 1989 low of 37%. Inspired by the revival of semiconductor companies, even manufacturers of vital chipmaking equipment are enjoying a resurgence.

In the face of an impending plant closure, the final summation that, "the industry will face the next decade in much better shape," rang hollow for us Utah plant employees, who would become the next victims of an industry fraught with problems. For us it would be an unfulfilled legacy.

## Final Activities

The administrative office areas were now dismantling. Partitions were coming down, and work areas were being gutted and cleaned up for eventual vacancy. As production operations shut down, the equipment was moved out and sent for temporary storage or disposal. As we walked the hallways, the sounds of carts and dollies of equipment were sometimes deafening. A sense of gut-wrenching finality hit us all as physical changes to the building occurred.

Fab operations, the last area to shut down production, was beginning to close off production starts. Before the first exits, which would shortly begin, the area held its last big shindig, a Thanksgiving dinner and party. Each shift held its own celebration, which on swing-shift culminated in someone creatively designing a turkey dart board with the company president's head located in the place of the turkey's. From the number of holes in the turkey, it appeared that more than a few people participated in this last open expression of hostility toward the company.

Realizing the futility of trying to combat these hostile feelings, Taylor and the remaining fab managers decided to take it all in stride with humor and aplomb. Taylor commented that it was much easier to feel like one of the fab employees, now that fab management was no longer compelled to represent the company perspective in such affairs. "I know how these employees feel, and I can relate to it myself," he said. Several of the off-shift supervisors had even participated in the dart throwing event; one of them put up the target board on her office wall. "It's a shame that it takes such a cataclysmic event to produce this kind of rapport," Taylor sadly mused.

The relief was evident as the remaining six hundred of us made final preparations to complete our tasks. A certain calmness and resignation had settled in as our energies refocused on the outplacement process. Little production remained at this point; most of our effort was targeted at finding meaningful ways to keep busy during the last few weeks. Many of us were counting down our last days in the plant and steeling ourselves for some lean times ahead.

## Implications

### Use Remaining Time Positively

Employees can use this final shutdown period to position themselves advantageously for future employment opportunities. If an employee has remained productive and made significant contributions throughout, he or she should request such verification from management in a letter of recommendation. Some employees at the Utah plant discovered that they had made a positive impression on a supervisor or coworker, who in turn was influential in getting them hired at another company. Employers will sense the attitude of workers who have recently experienced a reduction-in-force and will want to know about the employee's activities during that time. Furthermore, if work is available in areas of the plant where new skills may be acquired, employees may want to consider the possibility of reassignment to both help out production and receive marketable training. Managers and supervisors who help match production needs with employees' career interests will find a source of newly motivated workers who continue to care about their contributions.

### Adjust Work Load and Compensation

Compensation and work assignment practices may need to be reevaluated during this final stage. Often the workload will be unbalanced, and some areas will need to work and others will not. Although the Utah plant did not experience horseplay and sabotage, this is a time when some employees may decide to spend their idle hours at the plant playing pranks. Even more important, companies should not force employees to show up at the plant if no productive work is available. Employees with no reemployment plans who are also idle at work will tend to dwell upon the uncertainty and anxiety of their circumstances. If employees who want to work are given opportunities to do so, typically they won't resent others who prefer to stay at home. Pay considerations should be equitable and take into account those who are willing to complete needed tasks in this winding down period. Plant management should continue to allow local control of operations and decentralize decisions whenever possible.

*Plan Public Relations*

During this time, outside publicity is vital in helping draw the attention of prospective employers to the plant. Supervisors can suggest publicity events that will help to get community attention and provide employees with departure ceremonies to create memorable moments of their last days at the plant. Although job fairs require a great amount of organization and preparation, they promote employee relations and often result in effective placement opportunities. If the company is sponsoring an on-site outplacement center, most of the work involved in sponsoring job fairs can be done with the outplacement staff. If done ahead of the actual shutdown, the fair will not place an undue burden on the staff and will serve to publicize and foster more employment interest in plant employees.

Someone at the plant should be designated to focus on coordinating these public relations efforts. Press interest will revive, and outside businesses will solicit employees to take advantage of their services. Employees should not have to submit to unwanted solicitation at the plant. A public relations coordinator can help fend off undesired calls while making arrangements for community support services.

Companies facing plant downsizing should not shy away from reporting this event. In fact, companies should use publicity as a way to help employees advertise for future job prospects. Companies that try to avoid media attention will only trigger more negative reporting; the press will seek out stories from any willing source. If the "bad news" is anticipated and press releases are provided, the downsizing will become more than just another bad news story in the community. Report candidly and expeditiously through press releases the reasons for the downsizing, and continue to make public announcements as the process proceeds. Target specific media, and appeal to public concern for the plight of employees and their needs. Also, do not underreport the good news that unfolds as employees find reemployment and other companies step in to recruit prospective employees. If communications are planned and strategized, the company will not be continually forced into a defensive posture on the closure. Make public announcements about what the company is doing to help employees make the transition. Good public relations efforts will cast a more positive light on the company, and more important, they can help better position displaced employees to find other jobs.

The last plant communications meeting before their final departure can be particularly meaningful to employees. For most employees, this will be the last company forum to hear about how the company regards their contributions. If, as was the case at the Utah plant, employees have continued to make significant efforts to be productive and thereby have given the shutdown a positive cast in the community, management should publicize that fact both to employees and the community. Employees who are given an opportunity to feel proud of their accomplishments will tend to leave with a sense of having transcended an extremely painful experience.

Stage 8: Winding Down

| Employees | Management | Policymakers |
|---|---|---|
| —Remain a contributor<br>—Seek career training opportunities<br>—Be flexible in considering options<br>—Engage in sound financial planning | —Provide positive publicity<br>—Encourage departure ceremonies<br>—Match operations' needs with employees' desire for skill attainment | —Decentralize control to operations<br>—Maintain good ties with local management<br>—Provide resources and services including community support services |

# 14 December
## The End or Just the Beginning?

We had come a long way on this one-year journey. Many employees had moved on to exciting and fulfilling careers elsewhere, while many more of us waited with anticipation and some apprehension to actualize our future plans. No doubt the closure had taken its toll on personal lives, affecting income levels and creating family pressures. The reemployment process had been tough; many of us had abandoned established career paths in order to find new work. Some employees had never quite come to terms with the closure. They perceived it as the end of a selected vocation and a blow from which they would never really recover. Others had taken it all in stride, choosing not to look back and putting all resources into a successful transition elsewhere.

At the beginning of 1992, the plant population was 918 employees, averaging thirty-eight years old and mostly female (53 percent). Their average number of years with the company was about ten, and their average salary was about $23,245. The work force was made up of 71 percent nonexempt workers, 7 percent of whom were administrative; 60 percent manufacturing operators; and 33 percent technicians. Of the remaining 29 percent exempt personnel, 39 percent were engineers or technical people, and 61 percent were nontechnical white-collar workers.

By the final days of the closure in early December, the mix had changed considerably, indicating partly which of the employees had the easiest time negotiating earlier release dates to obtain other work. The population had now dwindled to about six hundred employees, 80 percent of whom were nonexempt and only 20 percent exempt. Of the nonexempt employees, 63 percent were manufacturing operators, 6 percent administrative workers, and 30 percent technicians. Only

28 percent of the exempt workers were engineers or technical people, 72 percent of the remaining exempt workers were nontechnical personnel. Clearly, exempt technical workers had been able to obtain employment most expeditiously; manufacturing operators had been least successful.

Local papers reported the final closing week of activities at the plant:

### Last Workers Punch Out

The last group of employees will hang up their smocks on Tuesday, signaling the demise of one of Utah's most prominent businesses. A cleanup crew of about 100 will work until March dismantling equipment and shipping it to other company plants. But the integrated circuit manufacturer's 26-year ride among the top employers in the county is over.

More importantly, the plant's closure is calculated in human terms. The closure swept through Signetics employment ranks like a hurricane-force wind, scattering employees in different directions. One employee, the manager of the characterization department at Signetics, had worked for the company for 16 years. He will punch his last time card today at Signetics and then report tomorrow to Eyring Corp., where he'll begin a new career as a radio frequency engineer/systems analyst. "I'm one of the lucky ones," he said. "There are still quite a few who are good professionals that are still looking."

## Exit Processing

The remaining task for the plant managers was to coordinate and conduct all final exit interviews and outprocessing for the last 600 employees. About 140 people would stay into 1993 on the closure crew, which left some 450 employees to exit in December. During the period from 8 December to 18 December, four days were designated for large group exit meetings. The logistics of organizing these groups proved problematic, because many of the supervisors had paid people though their last day and let them stay home. Contacting them all now would be difficult. Also, many of the supervisors and managers had already left for other jobs, leaving the task of contacting employees to those of us who remained.

An exit process consisting of a moving line of employees seemed most efficient: employees would walk from station to station—human resources, security, and health services; they would turn in all their company materials, be debriefed on benefits and health information, turn in company badges, and receive final paychecks. The payroll department was especially pressed by exit processing. There were only two people to make the final adjustments and calculations for hours worked, vacation accruals, and severance and bonus pay. Since supervisors had been less than conscientious in keeping accurate records and time cards, many of the paychecks were incorrect and had to be refigured. Even though payroll anticipated some problems, no one guessed the nightmare that would unfold on those last days of outprocessing.

Contributing to the problem was the surprise request from fab management to outprocess about 120 employees a week early. Only 25 percent of the fab employees were working, yet 85 percent of the rest of them were still coming to work, looking for things to do. The fab managers were concerned that these bored employees were wandering the hallways, disrupting what little work was going on. Brent was not pleased by requests to process these people early. "There is no reason why the fab couldn't have tried to be a little more accurate on their projections of when people would be finished up. They were the only area that had all of their people scheduled to go out on the same day, the fifteenth. They must have known that operations and processes would shut down in a sequential manner. They could have greatly simplified the administrative process in the beginning."

Further complicating the estimates of which employees were leaving and when were the last minute release date extensions being requested by supervisors. It would have been unrealistic to expect that all projects that needed to be completed before the closure would progress as planned. Nevertheless, as the final days drew to an end, managers scrambled to try to complete last-minute assignments. It was apparent, however, that, in some cases, the extensions requested were intended to provide a safety net for employees whose anticipated job offers had not yet come through. Jesse had stopped his job search several months earlier when he thought an offer from a local engineering and research company was coming. Expecting the offer any moment, he received a call from the new company asking him to sit in on a staff meeting. By the end of the discussion, he had a sinking feeling that something was not quite right: approval for the position to hire him had not come through. Trying not to panic, Jesse returned to the plant to try to resurrect some of his other job leads that he had abandoned. With just a few weeks before Christmas and his release date approaching on the fifteenth, he scrambled to make some contingency plans. After an appeal to human resources, he was granted an extension to 4 January to help him cope with some of his benefits difficulties and recover from what must have been a crushing blow to him and his family.

The plant was required to maintain accurate records of who was going out and when, and human resources tracked this information primarily through the receipt of the signed employee release date letters and extensions. Human resources was attempting to maintain files and records as final documentation on employees. In attempting to reconcile the receipt of the letters from people leaving in December, as opposed to those staying on with the closure crew through part of 1993, that department discovered that many employees had simply not bothered to sign and return their closure crew extension letters. These employees were contacted to ascertain whether they had chosen to stay on the closure crew or were leaving for another job. Corporate was strong-arming the plant to keep all records accurate and have the paperwork processed before the fifteenth, so as to be able to project the closing head count for 1992 and the beginning head count for 1993. Either not realizing or not being concerned about the additional burden they were placing on the plant at a very inopportune time, the corporate human resource department called to make sure that its demands would be complied with. Not even trying to conceal their displeasure with this lack of sensitivity, the plant human resource group begrudgingly put in the necessary overtime to comply with the seemingly arbitrary deadline.

During the last large group exits, it became apparent that payroll would not be able to issue final paychecks to these employees at the same time, despite best efforts to do so. These employees were told to return later that afternoon to pick up their checks or to provide proof of the need to change any errors on the checks that had been issued. Chaos prevailed when people returned early in the afternoon to pick up checks. Many did not expect to wait and came with small children, but they were again turned away when problems mounted and payroll fell farther behind. Most of the employees left, frustrated at having to come back the following day, but several chose to wait in the lobby, determined not to leave without check in hand. In the meantime, the two payroll employees tripped over themselves to get out checks for employees who had been waiting for hours. Some very rude and angry exchanges took place when some employees were told their wait was fruitless.

As payroll worked late into the night to catch up and prevent the same scene from recurring during the next group of exits, human resources contacted these employees to let them know when their paychecks would really be available. The additional financial burden of the approaching holidays made it difficult for the exiting employees to sympathize with administrative problems. By the fifteenth, checks were finally completed and distributed, thanks to the help of both Brent and the controller, who supervised the check distribution process in the lobby to avoid another check fiasco. Finally, employees were able to leave with checks in hand.

## Last Social Activities

The fab area held its farewell luncheon celebration on the fifteenth at a local dining hall. More than five hundred current and former employees, including some administrative support groups, showed up to experience what was to be the plant's last significant get-together. A quick introduction and note of appreciation was delivered by one of the fab managers, who then invited us to eat and make merry for the last time as a group of fellow employees. Cameras flashed, and people wandered around looking for particular coworkers to say their goodbyes to. One woman employee also worked the crowd as an Avon distributor, taking her last orders and collecting money on orders she had completed. Apparently, the plant had been a real gold mine for her. Not much emotion was evident during the affair; we all tried to remain upbeat in discussing each other's plans for school or reemployment. As we left the building, we each received a T-shirt—a final memento of our time with the company and an expression of appreciation for the extra effort during a very difficult year.

Some insights into the final days of the closure came in a farewell breakfast for people in some of the administrative groups who would stay through part of 1993. The breakfast was hosted by a parent company employee, a German citizen from one of the plants in Hamburg, who had been sent to the plant in January 1992 to help with the product and process transfers to other company sites. He recounted how impressed he had been with the Utah plant employees and the professionalism we had shown him during his one-year stay in Utah. He lauded the workers as more success-oriented than any he had ever known. He expressed his initial apprehension about how he would be received when he first came, knowing that he would be perceived as one of the enemy, taking away products from the plant. Yet he had experienced only cooperation and kindness from all with whom he had worked.

The plant controller, a transferee from corporate headquarters, had also come to the plant early in 1992 to help with the plant closure. He echoed the sentiments of the German manager, emphasizing that he had enjoyed his stay in Utah so much that he was going to try to seek reemployment in the state, right along with everyone else. He shared some anecdotes about how he had lately become a watchdog by whom employees passed if they wished to purchase plant furniture or equipment. Joking that he was also beginning to feel something like a used furniture dealer, he explained that he was required to tag desired items and collect money from employees as they left. Unfortunately, some employees had tried to sneak expensive company items out of the plant in file drawers and other furniture they had purchased. Someone had even managed to smuggle out the scales from the mail room, used to weigh letters for postage, much to the chagrin of the mail clerk.

We worked to complete last-minute projects and tie off loose ends, so we could go out with a sense of completion and accomplishment. By and large, the final week, hectic though it was, passed relatively smoothly. At this point, most of us had put the plant closure behind us and were caught up in the process of constructing our future.

## Implications

*Plan for an Efficient Exit*

Procedures for processing exiting employees should be planned well in advance (refer to May's implications). Contingency plans with backup support are advantageous, as we learned too late when glitches developed in processing final checks. Although this process need not be flawless, employees will not readily forgive major mishaps and unnecessarily long queue times. If possible, not all exits should be planned for the final day, but staggered over a period of time to coincide with area shutdowns. Rather than waiting in lines, employees can be contacted at home to come into the plant to complete the exit process. We discovered that supervisors and employees preferred to exit in work groups with their team members beside them. This provided some sense of comradery and comfort as co-workers left together.

# 15 Lessons Learned

Many of the steps we took in planning for the plant closure were both necessary and effective in preparing for the year that followed. While several of these steps or processes were straightforward and for the most part fulfilled their purposes, as the downsizing progressed there were some required interventions that were neither foreseen or facile in implementation.

## Preparing an Employee Retention Plan

One of the first concerns for the managers of a plant that is closing is how to retain key employees until the plant actually closes. This became a particular problem for our plant because we had a period of one year before the actual closure. Since the plant was a high-tech manufacturing facility, our technical and engineering people would be crucial to continued operation of the plant for the remaining year. At the same time, these were the people we knew would have the easiest time finding work elsewhere. The number of calls from headhunters to employees shortly after the closure announcement reinforced that concern. How would the company be able to provide enough incentive to these selected individuals to entice them to stay through the year, when they undoubtedly would be receiving attractive job offers from other companies?

The corporate staff, grappling with this issue, came up with a retention package that would apply to all employees who would remain until their completion dates. Given the plant employees' high average years of seniority with the company, the offer of double severance pay as a completion bonus seemed a reasonable retention package on the surface. As the plant staff began to review the list of key people for retention, however, it was clear that not all these individuals had enough time with the company to make this generic package attractive to them. At that time, the plant staff proposed that an additional retention bonus be applied for selected individuals on the list of key people. Since the corporate staff had already prepared a budget for spending on plant severance, there was initial apprehension about considering more money. After some negotiation, during which we provided evidence of the number of key people who were getting outside offers, the corporate staff finally relented. But they did insist on a cap for the number of people who would be offered the additional retention bonus. At the moment, this seemed reasonable, and the plant staff prepared to offer the special retention packages to certain individuals.

Despite the incentives given them, there were some key engineers that chose to accept other offers, leave the plant, and forfeit their bonuses. This was to be expected, given the higher security needs of some; it presented no real surprise to the plant staff. As these key people left, however, it then became important to retain those who would take their places. Rather than forfeit the amount budgeted for the people who left, the plant staff made a good case of being allowed to use discretion in allocating the plant retention bonus budget, so long as the forecast amount was not exceeded and employees were not added to the list who didn't meet the original criteria established for additional incentive consideration. As it turned out, about 70 percent of those designated to receive the additional retention bonus stayed to the end, making the program a vital factor in keeping critical employees.

One other consideration became essential in retaining employees. Virtually the entire engineering staff of one product division worked in the Utah plant. Originally, the plan was to offer most of these people offers to transfer to corporate headquarters in California. When it became evident that few, if any, would even consider relocation there because of the cost-of-living factors, the vice president prepared to resist providing financial provisions to make this move more attractive. When the engineering managers themselves told the vice president that they would not support a move unless the location was reconsidered, the vice president realized he faced the potential crisis of losing most, if not all, his engineering resources. The Utah engineering staff made him a proposal, which claimed that the New Mexico plant was the only real viable option for employees and sought further relocation incentives. After some heated discussion and negotiation over numbers and budget, corporate finally approved a plan that would facilitate transfer of nearly 85 percent of the original engineering group.

The most important element in planning for retention of employees proved to be the ability to negotiate. Budgeting finances is a vital aspect of the process and must be given due consideration. But at the same time, there must be budgetary leeway to accommodate issues that arise and the influence of market forces becomes well understood. It is very difficult to predict the willingness of individual families to transfer to other company sites or to assess group forces as a factor in influencing individual employees to remain behind with their coworkers and take their chances on finding other work later. Above all, it is crucial to understand and monitor the forces affecting displaced employees and their decisions to stay with the company or leave. Sometimes the rationale behind these decisions are not as logical as we may believe.

## Formulating an Effective Employee Communication Process

The plant staff anticipated that there would be numerous questions from employees needing to be addressed soon after the closure announcement. We formulated a schedule for the closure stages, including operations phasing down. Some preliminary written questions and answers enabled employees to begin to prepare for how the timing of reductions-in-force would affect them. We held meetings with all employees on each shift to review the information and elicit further concerns and issues the employees might raise. We researched answers to the questions raised in the meetings to provide timely responses to employees. Since most of the first wave of employee concerns dealt with benefits-related issues, meetings were held within a week to provide information on this topic alone. Each month, employee communications meetings were held; along with the monthly operation meetings, these kept the employees abreast of any new developments.

The employee communication meetings proved an invaluable means of keeping in touch with employees' feelings and allowing employees to express their fears and problems and seek affirmation that they were not alone in their troubles. Because each group sought the same reassurances and information on how the company would support them, the meetings also served to break down barriers between management and workers. As time passed, the meetings became less useful as an information tool and more beneficial as a venue for employees to air their frustrations. Sometimes just the sense of gathering as a group, in which many others were fighting the same battles, comforted people.

As questions were asked and answers communicated, an information packet took shape. Many employees asked the same questions at different times, so the packet became a tool to ensure some consistency was maintained. There was a real effort to answer all questions, in a timely way, and to minimize misinformation. The information packet became an ad hoc downsizing policy manual and was very helpful to supervisors who fielded the many questions.

We learned that communication was crucial in helping employees cope during this very difficult period. If employees are to make good decisions about their plans, finances, and development opportunities, timely and relevant information is vital. Communication must be frequent, open and honest, and should allow for give and take. The easiest way to build resentment is to try to bluff an answer to a question. Employees need to know that they can share their troubles and even have an influence on how the company addresses them. Many good suggestions came from employees and were put to use in the closure process.

Management must take pains to focus communication on what matters most to the employees. Any self-serving behavior by management will trigger instant hostility and distrust and lead toward a downward spiral of productivity and morale. Depending on the stage of the reductions-in-force, once this occurs, there may never be a chance to recover. We learned that managers and workers pulling together and working as a team during the downsizing can prove to

be both cathartic and liberating, providing each with a sense of empowerment and accomplishment. Not only did this cooperation help
employees weather difficult times, it provided them some leverage in
securing reemployment; it helped make a success out of what most
would consider a disaster.

One area about which the company failed to communicate effectively involved forecasting work schedules and manpower needs.
Some good people left early when they grew frustrated at not knowing or being told when they could expect their release dates. In some
cases, this was unavoidable. But more often than not, a date could
easily have been projected early on, which would have avoided both
the need for negotiations and the mounting anxiety about the unknown. Although we in management could not have prevented individual extensions beyond release dates, we certainly could have done
a better job of keeping these more to a minimum than was the case.
Particularly in the fab operation, more initial effort in planning and
communicating with employees to project area phase-downs and the
subsequent need for certain job functions may have precluded the
need to send some people home early with pay to wait out their
release dates. This would have prevented a major morale problem.

## Providing Outplacement and Retraining Services

The plant staff sought and obtained approval from corporate to provide both outplacement and retraining services to employees. We recognized the comfort these services would provide, so this was one of
the first announcements we made to employees after the announcement of the closure. As part of the closure schedule given to employees, the retraining program was to start up the following month
and continue throughout the year, as the need was manifest. A formal on-site outplacement center would open at the same time the
first operation began to shut down. This allowed enough time for the
employees to begin to assess their career interests and needs before
targeting specific jobs.

As the first step in preparing employees to seek reemployment,
classes were offered in career management, job-search strategies, interviewing, and preparing a résumé. The plan was to offer these

classes to all employees and give them the tools they needed to complete their résumés. An on-line system was set up to allow employees to enter their résumés on a computer and to eventually transfer them to the outplacement center for refinement and printing. Although some employees chose to delay taking the class, eventually nearly 85 percent of all employees attended the outplacement training classes.

Next we administered a retraining needs assessment survey to determine the type of training most employees desired. This was coordinated with a local college technology center to pinpoint employees' interests and match them to the kinds of jobs available in the local market. Because of the constraints of the retraining budget allowance, the classes were targeted to support the greatest employee needs. Most of the classes requested and scheduled were computer software and programming classes. Since not all the employees' needs would be covered by these classes we found it necessary to offer an additional program to provide flexibility for the few employees who identified different career paths. Through this program, called *career reimbursement*, employees received $600 as a reimbursement pool if they could provide evidence of another kind of training or educational program that led to their targeted career objective. Through these two retraining services, all employees could benefit from retraining tailored to fit their individual needs. Both programs were used extensively by the plant employees.

Even though the on-site outplacement center was used more selectively, it was also deemed a success. Although most employees found jobs through means other than the center (mainly through networking with former employees or friends), the center was useful in providing résumé services and coaching and counseling to employees who were not confident of their job-search abilities. The center served mainly to promote the company's work force to other employers and greatly heightened the community's awareness of the plant's impending reductions-in-force. By acting as a focal point for employment information and contacts, the center became a convenient place for employees to pursue job searches. The good will the center generated, both among employees and in the community, gave the company a public relations boost.

Although some graveyard shift employees complained about the lack of availability of the retraining classes and outplacement center on their shift, these services were certainly the greatest single factor in helping employees work through the stress and anxiety of the closure. We achieved this advantage through early negotiations with corporate to obtain a liberal budget for these services. Our research and effort to make a case for such services paid off handsomely, for both the company and the employees. This is one function that companies planning for plant downsizing cannot afford to treat lightly. If at all possible, companies should err on being too liberal and offering too many services to employees. In the long run, the associated gains far outweigh the expenses.

## Staying in Touch with the Community

The Utah community where the plant was located was unique in some respects. The plant was a major employer in the valley and contributed significantly to the city's tax base. Also, some years earlier, when a steel plant in the valley had shut down forcing thousands of workers on unemployment, a groundswell of community support led to finding a buyer for this factory, restarting operations, saving the jobs of the majority of workers, and eventually making the plant a profitable venture. This experience, along with the potential loss of income from our plant to the city, motivated the local economic development board, including the mayor, to try to salvage the Utah semiconductor plant through a similar process.

A special committee consisting of local politicians and businessmen put together a strategy to keep the semiconductor plant alive. As a member of the local economic board, Brent was asked to be on this committee, along with several plant employees who would represent the workers' interests. Although the circumstances of our plant closure were much different than those of the local steel mill, there was a lot of optimism and energy behind the community effort to save the plant. Despite its failure to keep the plant open, not all the committee's actions were in vain. Steps taken to find a buyer and other actions originating in this committee allowed plant management to have a voice in and, in some cases become an advocate for, the kind of community outreach support and visibility that would later help employees find reemployment.

When the plant closure became inevitable, the networking produced by the committee's work was invaluable in attracting services needed in the outplacement process. The positive public relations achieved in having community leaders work with the plant also generated some favorable press coverage for the company and the employees. Contacts were made at high levels of the state government, where some lobbying on behalf of the company sought to secure federal funding that would allow the employees significant benefits for schooling and unemployment. Because of all the community attention and visibility, the plant management team was able to get the company to provide additional funding for employees when the need arose. It seemed that no one wanted to say no to the plant.

Finally, these joint efforts within the community convinced the employees that the company was doing everything it could do on their behalf. When the time finally came for the reductions-in-force, employees left with mostly good feelings toward the company, especially toward plant management. Without doubt, the positive attitudes of the employees as they left would play a major role in their efforts to successfully find other work.

Undoubtedly, the Utah plant had many factors working on its behalf within the local community. Most other companies may not be so fortunate. Companies that do not have the same positive relationships in the community must make constant efforts to work with community leaders and politicians to help with downsizing issues. Company donations toward community support efforts should be considered. A high-level company or plant representative should be designated to sit in on joint business-community meetings to offer perspective and to be an advocate for displaced workers. As the final downsizing period approaches, arrangements should be made for state unemployment services representatives to hold meetings in the plant with all employees to let them know about services and resources available within the community for unemployed workers. Finally, if some services deemed important to the employees—such as career testing and counseling, financial counseling, and employment referral services—are not available within the community, the company should make every effort to either organize those services within the community or offer the services itself.


## Managing the Unknown

Not surprisingly, our company, failed to pay attention to events not anticipated. This is an aspect of planning which most other companies faced with plant downsizing or closure also neglect. For example, if at the outset the plant had forecasted a specific work schedule, by operation, and revised it as needed, there could have been more precise planning of release dates for employees. This would have avoided morale problems, such as paying people for no work or holding employees up from obtaining other jobs. As it was, only a general schedule had been created at the point notification letters were sent to employees. Consequently, extension letters, rather than adjustments of release dates at some earlier point, became necessary. Careful thought should go into planning for contingencies, such as how exceptions to policy may be regarded and treated. The company received many requests from employees for exceptions to continue working beyond their release dates. Each request evoked prolonged debate among managers. Guidelines could be spelled out and communicated in advance. With some forethought to granting exceptions, some rules of thumb would permit a smoother decision process and a less volatile atmosphere between management and workers.

Another process that could have been implemented more smoothly was the relocation of transferring employees to the New Mexico site. Before the actual relocation period, only a very cursory relocation policy and procedures handbook were produced. This did nothing but foster questions and attempts by individual employees to negotiate with both the corporate and plant human resource departments. Complicating matters further was the inconsistency in the answers from each of the relocation representatives at the three different company sites. Had issues and potential problems been more carefully evaluated and dealt with earlier in the process, there would have been less need for individual counseling and problem-solving as the relocations were occurring. To its credit, the company did establish a relocation task force to try to expedite the problems employees encountered as they proceeded to relocate. But if a committee had been formed earlier in the process, before actual relocations, much confusion and frustration could have been avoided.

Finally, some of the plant's problems with employee theft and unauthorized use of company property could have been avoided. The process used to track property passes to employees was sorely inadequate; it should have been revamped long before the need to retrieve company property became apparent. With early anticipation, a system could have been set up to control property coming and going from the plant. Some theft would have been likely, regardless of careful control measures, but much more could have been done to discourage dishonesty and solicit cooperation among employees. Although the company did not experience much employee sabotage, companies that announce reductions-in-force or closures must be prepared to take measures to avoid or control this problem as well.

Obviously no company or manager can be expected to anticipate and plan for every contingency that may occur during a plant downsizing. Nevertheless, measures can and should be taken early in the process to avoid potential problems. A task force can be established to look into areas where problems might arise and plan as much as possible for contingencies. Assign probabilities to each potential problem, and take steps to avoid the problems or minimize their impact. Above all, the plant managers should be prepared to deal with exceptions to and deviations from the expected course of events. A number of planning models and tools are commercially available to help managers deal with contingency planning. One lesson our managers learned was to be flexible and not rely too heavily on precedent. As the plant manager himself stated, a plant closure can sometimes be extremely liberating for a manager considering the best course of action.

## Downsizing Issues

Although many issues surfaced in the plant during the one-year closure period, only a few warrant general discussion: relocating large numbers of employees to other company sites; managing the issue of consistency versus fairness regarding bonus consideration and job accommodations; maintaining positive morale and productivity to the end; helping employees manage the transition and adaptive period; and determining the locus of control on decisions affecting plant employees.

### Relocating Employees to Other Sites

If large numbers of employees are going to be relocated to other company sites out of state when a plant closes, the company should anticipate certain issues. Employees will want to communicate with a central person, someone who will be both attentive and responsive to their concerns and fears about moving. They will want to be briefed on the new environment to which they are moving and be allowed to take their families to investigate the new area. Some employees will have special family needs or personal interests that need to be addressed. There will also be a need to distinguish between the considerations the employee will be responsible for and those the company will be responsible for. Last, employees and their families will have general anxiety about relocating, and this may become an issue, depending on how it is handled and the strength of the support systems.

The company would be wise to appoint a relocation move coordinator who will be a central contact for employees and ensure some consistency in how relocations are managed. By having one point of contact, the employee can be assured that he or she is not alone in the concerns and problems that loom ahead. This central person can also give feedback on how others are doing and suggest resources that may address the specific needs of families. At the suggestion of our coordinator, we initiated seminars on moving for the whole family; they provided useful information on what a family might expect from the move, along with tips for making the move more positive.

The relocating employees themselves can form a powerful support system to help facilitate the relocation process. Encouraging relocating families to get together informally and get acquainted can help establish invaluable contacts that will greatly foster a sense of community within the group. An informal relocation newsletter, sponsored either by the company or by the relocatees, can provide useful information and tips on the relocation process and offer suggestions to employees on what works well and what does not. Sometimes this information is more valuable to relocating employees than any the company might provide.

Depending on the new location and availability of housing, families may have problems finding adequate temporary living arrangements. If at all feasible, the company can intervene and negotiate with realtors to secure temporary arrangements as a block, with a specified number of units and a time commitment. This approach necessitates prior awareness of employees' housing needs through data-gathering. In the long run, families have one less headache to contend with, and the arrangements can prove very cost effective for both the employee and the company.

## Consistency and Equity Concerns

Employees made a number of special requests during the closure period that raised the issue of how to maintain equitable treatment of all employees in the plant and still accommodate special circumstances or needs. Typically the requests were related to bonus and severance consideration or job accommodations to allow for new employment negotiations. For example, the Design Six engineers had managed to secure employment quickly after the announcement was made. Up to that point, no release dates had been established. Each of these employees asked that he be granted a sixty-day release date at the time of the request. This was troublesome for management, who had not yet forecast the need for the engineers' work, and it advanced the concern that other employees, once they found employment, would want to follow suit. The company could simply have turned down the request on the grounds that if management allowed any individuals to negotiate special deals, there would be no end to them. The need for a general guideline on this issue quickly became apparent.

Fear of potential class action suits and litigation looms large in the mind of an experienced manager. Normally this fear is well grounded and is good cause for circumspect decision making. Nevertheless, circumstances in a plant downsizing or closure are not and should not be considered normal business operating procedure. Individuals will lobby hard for their interests, especially during a difficult time when easy answers and rational decisions are not appreciated. Management has more to lose by being overly conservative and taking only prudent risks than by striving to be more compassionate about the needs of the employee. Granted, me-too employee requests will follow whenever an exception to normal practice is allowed. Management must nevertheless weigh the pros and cons of each request and rule on the specific merits of each case. Despite legal counsel (undoubtedly received from corporate headquarters) to take a hard line and be consistent on policy administration, management must share employees' perspectives and give consideration to the individual employee.

As the downsizing progresses and needs for employee work change, so will the need to review prior positions on policy or practice. It may be more practical to arrange for job accommodation requests later in the downsizing process than earlier. Employees should understand this and try as much as possible to bring their personal needs in line with those of the plant. Employees who fail to heed business realities and department needs should pay the consequences when they advance their separate requests for special treatment. In general, both employees and legal services will regard business needs as legitimate guidelines in determining whether to grant individual employee requests involving exceptions to policy. Managers should be especially careful to ensure that requests are not refused or granted on the basis of illegal discriminatory factors such as age, sex, race, or disability.

Finally, managers should be prepared to provide the rationale for each ruling on individual employee requests. These considerations should involve a group of managers so as to better represent all viewpoints, and ensure that each decision meets the "reasonable person" rule. This may not guarantee that fault won't be found with the decisions, but it certainly will increase the chances that employees will find the rulings to be equitable.

### Maintaining Morale and Productivity

Depending on the length of the downsizing period, it may be a struggle to maintain previous levels of employee morale and productivity. As was the case at our plant, as soon as the employee discovered that his or her work was fruitless and would not lead to future returns, that person tended to stop putting forth an honest effort.

This will be more true among some employees than others, but it is a real factor once reductions-in-force announcements are made. Since our plant closure period was rather extended, this became a significant problem, given that product schedules were to continue as normal for some time. The plant endured a short period after the closure announcement during which both morale and productivity suffered initially, then rebounded. Once the reality set in, the plant experienced several months of almost business-as-usual atmosphere. Then, as the final weeks approached, morale and productivity took a turn for the worse.

Since morale and productivity tend to have a linear relationship, management should focus on building a positive work climate. By fostering a climate of support, particularly for employees who are experiencing difficulties, plant managers can help create a sense of community among employees that will allow them to vent their frustrations and share fears and concerns about the future. Team meetings are a good forum to discuss these concerns. It is important that employee concerns not be taken for granted or deprecated in any way. Informal get-togethers within work groups or departments can be encouraged, if not actively organized, by the company. These informal parties can provide an upbeat climate with the right balance of work and distraction and can be very cathartic. Recognition committees can plan activities to celebrate continued examples of excellent performance during the downsizing process. Award ceremonies, if appropriate, can also help to maintain the sense of accomplishment and employee achievements.

As employees cope with increasing family and financial pressures, flexible work arrangements should be considered as a way to provide some slack. If necessary, additional compensation programs may be instituted to encourage productivity or work attendance—Signetics was able to offer an enhanced overtime pay program to provide incentives to employees who were required to put in additional hours to accomplish scheduled production needs. Supervisors need to be especially sensitive to the special needs of their employees. If employees are treated with respect and provided sound incentives, supervisors can be the most effective tool to ensure that employee morale will be maintained until the end.

*Managing the Transitions and Adaptive Process*

Each employee ultimately found his or her own way to cope with the plant closure. Some employees had a relatively easy adjustment period, with no apparent regrets or negative feelings about their situation. At the other extreme, many employees continued to have difficulty coming to terms with the closure and its impact on their lives. These employees faced more stress and anxiety as they resigned themselves to circumstances they didn't like. They felt helpless to pull themselves out of a cycle of bitterness and despair. Most employees went through a transition process that began with initial shock and denial and progressed to making changes and plans that would lead to new beginnings. This transition process is not unlike what people experience when a serious disease or death occurs in the family (see Figure 1).

Interestingly, these stages seemed almost to correspond by month with the events that took place during the final year. After the announcement in January, most people were astounded and struggled to recover from the shock of the news. Through February, most employees felt some degree of anger and hostility toward the company or plant that would do such a thing to them. In March, employees made every attempt to bargain and negotiate with the company to ensure that they would receive all available benefits and special offers, assurances of what they could expect if they stayed with the

*Figure 1.* Stages of Employee Response to Plant Downsizing

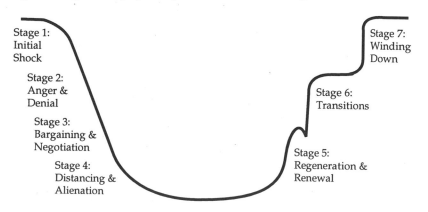

Stage 1:
Initial
Shock

Stage 2:
Anger &
Denial

Stage 3:
Bargaining &
Negotiation

Stage 4:
Distancing &
Alienation

Stage 5:
Regeneration &
Renewal

Stage 6:
Transitions

Stage 7:
Winding
Down

company to the end. By April, a number of events and experiences at the plant had left many employees feeling alienated and distanced from each other, from management, and from the company. From that time until late June, the plant experienced its lowest point in both morale and productivity.

Perhaps the turning point came when job prospects and recruiting efforts by other electronics firms were advertised or promoted through the outplacement center. Hiring activity had always tended to pick up each year in the late spring and early summer when families were more willing to move. Maybe the advent of summer helped pull employees out of their despair and gave them renewed hope and energy. It might even have been the plant's focus on recognition and morale-building activities in June that contributed to the renewal process. No matter the cause, after that point only a few employees continued to suffer from inertia and disillusionment.

July brought with it the first set of departing employees, primarily those who were relocating to the New Mexico plant. As the engineering services area began to shut down operations in August, employees began to reconcile themselves either with unemployment or new employment elsewhere. Not until September did most of the remaining employees confront the consequences of their actions, plans, and decisions or their failure to take steps. At this vantage point, they knew full well that they could no longer postpone facing the future. As October activities in the plant commemorated its history and provided employees a last glimpse into their past with the company, many employees found that nostalgia can bring both acceptance and reconciliation. At times, however, when employees watched others leave, they realized their own lack of preparation, and remembering happier times at the plant, some employees momentarily reexperienced the pain and grief of the downsizing process.

Efforts by plant managers in the final months of November and December showed particular sensitivity to employee needs. In order to help employees through the final period, each area of the plant tried to be more flexible and understanding as the last of the work was completed and work demands diminished. In many cases, local area celebrations and informal discussions with coworkers and supervisors helped provide a outlet for frustrations and anxieties and facilitated networking. The last plant communications meeting reinforced the great efforts and success of plant employees to the end. Almost everyone felt a sense of relief and comradery that we had all made it through.

By helping employees understand and become aware of the transition process and stages they will experience, companies can contribute to a healthier and speedier adjustment period for most employees. This education can also help them discern what is normal and what is not. If counseling resources are available from the beginning (our company offered these through our employee assistance program and through classes on managing transitions), employees will tend less to feel victimized and blame the company for their troubles. Couseling will also help them feel empowered and to become more proactive in dealing with the necessary business of reemployment.

### Locus of Control on Policy and Procedures

In a plant the size of ours (900 employees in four operations areas), the issue of locus of control may arise. Should every decision concerning the downsizing be made centrally by plant management? Or should some control and decisions rest with separate operational areas within the plant? This can be a difficult issue and can turn volatile when employees decide they don't like an answer they get from one of the sources. In the extreme, departments can turn against each other, which leads to general confusion and disharmony in the plant.

A plant steering committee, where each area is represented, can create a forum for discussion of issues that affect plant policy and practice. At Signetics, this group was most effective when meetings were held regularly and all members attended. In the beginning, meetings might be as often as two or three times a week. Later on, as the number of significant issues and questions decline, a weekly or biweekly meeting may be sufficient. The steering committee should decide which issues have broad, plantwide implications and need central control and which issues don't affect other parts of the plant. Those issues that affect only specific operational areas may be returned to the departments for local decision-making and control.

Some examples of the type of issues that may surface where locus of control becomes relevant are time-off practices, work schedules, pay practices, recognition activities, safety and health practices, and release dates, extensions, and special requests. The issues of pay and safety and health practices had far-reaching impact on the plant and therefore were decided centrally. Issues such as time off, work schedules, and recognition activities can be determined at the local department level, although some plantwide coordination may need to take place. In regard to release dates, extensions, and special requests, the plant found that general policy and guidelines needed to be set by the central plant steering committee, but interpretation could be made case by case by local area management.

Some factors that may be relevant when determining locus of control are timing and implementation. At the beginning of the downsizing period, it is important that areas show unity and consistency in applying policy. It is at this point that most of the important downsizing issues will surface and be decided. Later, as areas slow down and issues become more mundane, local areas should be given maximum control to manage in order to respond best to their employees' needs. If the implementation of a policy or practice appears problematic, each area should be given discretion in how best to carry out the particular decision. If employees are given a chance to influence something they feel is important to them, they will more readily support the decisions that are made. In general, the more discretion that can be given to local areas, the more positive and supportive these areas will be on downsizing decisions and the more positive employees will feel about their reduction-in-force experience overall.

Table 1. Downsizing and Closure Implications Summary

| Stage | Employees | Management | Policymakers |
|---|---|---|---|
| Initial Shock | —Take time to grieve<br>—Challenge downsizing or closure assumptions<br>—Ask policy and impact questions<br>—Maintain productivity | —Hold open forum discussions with employees<br>—Respond honestly to questions<br>—Compile issues/concerns list<br>—Formulate release date plan to match operations shutdown | —Consider options to downsizing or closure<br>—Provide referral services<br>—Formulate severance/benefits package for employees<br>—Be familiar with plant downsizing and closure literature (best practices)<br>—Have an operations shutdown plan<br>—Establish trust and confidence in local plant management |
| Anger and Denial | —Try to diffuse emotions<br>—Talk with other employees<br>—Don't displace anger to other victims<br>—Seek understanding and clarity about downsizing ramifications | —Clarify information; respond to rumors<br>—Be more available; encourage frequent communication<br>—Provide early intervention for unusually troubled employees<br>—Don't engage in blaming<br>—Express confidence in employees and provide encouragement | —Prepare key employee retention packages<br>—Consider productivity incentives |
| Bargaining and Negotiations | —Understand available options both within company and outside<br>—Try to understand company viewpoint<br>—Explore career alternatives<br>—Test organizational boundaries<br>—Provide input to management on concerns and problems | —Represent employees' concerns<br>—Help formulate and present proposals to company<br>—Seek out majority and minority employee opinions on process and direction<br>—Understand employees' perceptions | —Allow some plant discretion in applying policy during downsizing or closure<br>—Consider plant proposals<br>—Be clear about nonnegotiables |

*Table 1.* Continued

| Stage | Employees | Management | Policymakers |
|---|---|---|---|
| Distancing and Alienation | —Resist tendency to withdraw<br>—Try to re-energize and find meaning through networks<br>—Avoid counterproductive venting<br>—Try to match interests of company and self | —Identify inadequacies in policy<br>—Avoid contributing to withdrawal and alienation<br>—Ensure appropriate attention from company<br>—Maintain dialogue with employees and corporate representatives | —Provide company liaison to plant<br>—Ensure frequent and ongoing contact with plant<br>—Resist tighter control<br>—Avoid business-as-usual attitude |
| Regeneration and Renewal | —Engage in contingency planning—exercise creative options<br>—Look for success patterns and learn from other employees' experiences<br>—Establish networks and contacts both inside and outside plant | —Help facilitate networking and cross-fertilization<br>—Allow job searching on company time<br>—Share personal strategies with employees<br>—Celebrate employee successes<br>—Develop an effective exiting process | —Help to forge community contacts and alliances<br>—Pursue all available funding sources<br>—Collect employee need information |
| Transitions | —Take advantage of services provided<br>—Prepare for departures of friends and coworkers<br>—Avoid complacency<br>—Be engaged in career plans and new skill acquisition | —Help manage and encourage use of outplacement services<br>—Tailor services to specific needs<br>—Make work rearrangements to cover operations and cross-train employees | —Provide adequate outplacement services<br>—Allow flexibility in operation coverage<br>—Concentrate on community and public relations support |
| Winding Down | —Remain a contributor<br>—Seek career training opportunities<br>—Be flexible in considering options<br>—Engage in sound financial planning | —Provide positive publicity<br>—Encourage departure ceremonies<br>—Match operations' needs with employees' desire for skill attainment | —Decentralize control to operations<br>—Maintain good ties with local management<br>—Provide resources and services including community support services |

# Epilogue

One month after I left the plant in December 1992, I bumped into Taylor at a local fast food restaurant. He was on his lunch break from the plant. "How are things going at the plant?" I inquired.

"It's pretty slow, and the people left are getting anxious about what will happen to them," he replied. "You left at a good time. I'm trying to do whatever they need at this point so that I can leave for Arizona in February with a clear conscience."

Shirley would remain at the plant, transitioning from her human resources position to work at the outplacement center. She had been granted her wish to stay until the very end, which turned out to be the middle of May 1993. She still had the same energy and verve as she talked about helping to place the remaining employees: "It's kind of lonely around here, but it's fun to see people find jobs and readjust." She became the last contact most employees would have with the plant, keeping the last spirit of community alive as she exchanged information on former plant employees. Now, the informal networking and contacts among friends would become the only legacy of a once vibrant community of plant employees.

# Appendixes

The materials included in these appendixes are actual resource material we used at various stages of the plant closure. "Questions and Answers" was formulated in response to the number and types of questions asked by employees during the first few months. It is numbered by the sequence in which the questions were raised and grouped by topical areas. In addition to "Questions and Answers," I have included the worker adjustment information packet, "Being out of Work Doesn't Mean Being out of Opportunities," the Employee Release Date Letter and Retention Bonus Letter.

# Appendix 1: Questions and Answers on the Plant Closure By Topic

Benefits, Final Payout, Job Opportunities, Release Dates, Relocation, Retirement, Training, Unemployment, General

NOTICE: We are answering these questions based upon the best information available. If any amendments are required, you will be notified. In all cases, the Benefit Summary Plan descriptions will be the final determination.

## Benefits

Q42  Will there be a benefits change window?

A42  Normal windows apply, however, please see the benefits supervision if you have a specific problem. We have made arrangements to handle specific individual issues. We ask that you bring any such concerns to us by February 15.

*Vacation Cap, Service Dates/Recognition*

Q28  Will years of service be just at the plant or both the parent company and plant years combined?

A28  For all purposes other than pension they are combined when no breaks in service occurred or if you were a RIF [reduction-in-force] and returned within one year, or voluntarily quit and returned within 30 days. Past service is also credited once an employee has been continuously re-employed for six years. The crediting of past service for pension purposes follows a different set of rules. Contact Benefits for more specific information.

Q30  We may experience problems with vacation caps and anniversary bonus vacations, i.e., we may need employees to work even though their vacation hours will be capping and their anniversary bonus deadlines are coming up. Can we make exceptions?

A30    As a result of the plant closure, the vacation cap as well as the anniversary vacation deadline have both been dropped.

Q71    If an employee who had prior service came back but has returned for less than 6 years, will they lose prior service?

A71    Yes, because credit for past service can only occur after six (6) years for purposes other than pension. Pension credit has different rules; contact Benefits if you have questions about that.

Q159    If employees return for less than six years, could it be waived like they did five-year vesting?

A159    The current policy requiring an employee to be hired for six years in order for previous service to be bridged remains in affect and is not changed.

Q121    Does the company still plan to give Service Recognition awards?

A121    Yes, we will begin to order 1992 awards within a few weeks. Awards presentations will be on a quarterly basis rather than issuing all awards in the fall. Supervisors will be given more details as awards are ordered.

Q122    If an employee goes to work for an affiliate company after termination does the employee retain seniority and benefits at current level? What if they go to work for an affiliate company a year after the separation date?

A122    Whether or not an employee rehired by another company plant would have bridging of all service and benefit entitlements would depend on the policies at the gaining organization.

Q157    If you are out on MLOA [Medical Leave of Absence] during your anniversary date, will that affect your date?

A157    No.

*ESP [Employee Savings Plan] (401k)*

Q35    ESP. Will you provide us with documentation on our options?

A35    Yes. Information will be provided by Friday, 24 January '92. If you require other information, please contact Benefits for assistance.

Q69    Can I change my ESP deductions?

A69    Yes, per the provisions of the plan; i.e., once every six months. Please see Human Resources.

Q75    What are my options for my 401k plan upon termination?

A75    Employees whose balance is less than $3500 will receive a distribution. Other employees can elect a distribution or defer distribution until age 65. Employees who receive a distribution can likely "roll over" the money to another qualified program and defer any tax liability. You should seek individual counsel regarding the best alternative for you.

Q78    What about options to rollover my 401k monies?

A78    We recommend you contact a bank, broker or other individual consultant to discuss how this can be accomplished and what investment options may be available.

Q91    Are there any circumstances under which an employee can receive their ESP money prior to age 59 1/2 and not incur a 10% federal and a possible additional state penalty?

A91    There may be special provisions under death and disability which may affect this.

Q92    Can a plant closure be classified as a financial hardship in applying for ESP funds?

A92    No. All employees will be able to receive a distribution of their accounts after termination. Until then, normal withdrawal provisions will apply.

Q93    If ESP funds are deferred, why can't the age rule of 59 1/2 be used to withdraw funds?

A93    The ESP plan requires that, if distribution is deferred at termination, the account must remain in the plan until age 65. Employees who think they might want access to their accounts prior to age 65 should take the distribution at termination and roll it over into an IRA (Individual Retirement Account). Under current rules, funds can be withdrawn from IRAs after age 59 1/2 without penalty for early withdrawal.

Q94    Will our last payoff check have ESP deducted in order to help us from the tax sharks?

A94    ESP will be deducted only from the "wages" portion of your final check. ESP will not be taken from severance or completion bonus.

Q160   What mutual funds did the company invest in during 1991?

A160   A copy is posted on each ESP Awareness bulletin board.

*LOA & STD [Leave of Absence & Short-Term Disability]*

Q76    If an employee goes on medical leave of absence and remains out past the plant closure, will disability benefits continue?

A76    Yes, until you are released by your doctor or until the maximum benefit period is reached—whichever comes first.

Q148   What if I'm on MLOA and receive my 60-day notice, will my short-term disability continue or 26 weeks? What if I receive my 60-day notice and then go out on MLOA, will my benefits continue for 26 weeks?

A148   If your disability occurred before your final release date, your short-term disability will continue until released by your doctor or until you exhaust your benefits, whichever comes first.

*LTD [Long-Term Disability]*

Q73    Can I stop my Long-Term Disability deductions?

Q73    Yes, please contact Benefits.

*EAP [Employee Assistance Program]*

Q56    If an employee feels they need counseling to deal with the stresses of the plant closure is counseling available?

A56    Yes, the normal Employee Assistance Program worked through Benefits can provide this service.

*Medical Insurance/COBRA*

Q43     Will COBRA benefits be available?

A43     Yes.

Q113    Why are the COBRA insurance rates so high with Metropolitan and why weren't we told earlier about the high cost?

A113    Rates are determined by our experience. We are currently looking into possible other alternatives.

Q111    I understand that there is a law that an employer must carry an employee for 30 days on medical insurance?

A111    The WARN Act requires 60 days notice which includes insurance coverage as long as the employee works out the notice. Benefits continuation is available under COBRA. This process and the costs were discussed at the employee meetings. If you need more information, please contact employee benefits.

Q112    What if you are pregnant and due after termination; would the insurance still pay or it since it's a preexisting condition?

A112    Yes, providing you continue coverage under COBRA. Any services provided after you insurance coverage ends are not covered, even if the condition being treated began while you were employed.

Q114    Will the company allow outside insurance companies the opportunity to offer a "Group Plan" to the large number of displaced people we will have? Two or three of them bidding for this windfall will drive the premium price far below what the COBRA plan would cost?

A114    We are currently exploring to see if this is a possibility.

*Holidays*

Q117    Since the closure year ends 12/15/91, can the two holidays 12/24 and 12/25 be moved to earlier in the year, like Thanksgiving?

A117    No. The target is to close the plant by 12/15/91, however, there will be significant clean-up activity during these regularly scheduled holidays.

Q145    In response to the answer to question 117, it seems quite unfair that employees would be expected to work up until December 15 but forfeit the two holidays in December. If I remember right, each plant had the option to determine when they would take their 10 holidays during the year. Why can't we adjust the holiday schedule so that the December holidays are moved to earlier dates, like July 24?

A145    Alternatives were considered and the decision made to retain our current holiday schedule. There are no changes contemplated at this moment.

*Final Payout*

Q       What about completion bonus for MLOA's?

A       Employees RIF'd on MLOA will be entitled to severance pay but not to any completion bonus. Severance/completion bonus arrangements will be handled on a case-by-case basis.

Q4    What happens if I decide to quit now or sometime before the end of my assignment?

A4    Basically, a voluntary resignation is no different now than before. You'll be entitled to pay earned to date of termination and pay-off of unused vacation and PTO time. You would not be eligible for any severance or completion incentives.

Q5    What do I get if I stay to "the end of my assignment"?

A5    You would of course receive pay earned and any unused vacation/ PTO time. Each employee will receive at least sixty (60) days notice of his/her specific assignment completion date. In addition, you will re- ceive severance pay according to policy and a completion incentive payment in the same amount as your severance pay.

Q16   How do you determine an employee's severance pay?

A16   Two weeks for every three years of service or fraction thereof per Pol- icy 501 in P3 Manual.

Q18   If we give 60 days written notice but do not need an employee to be here physically, can they leave early? Can we give them severance but not the completion bonus?

A18   There is no provision for pay in lieu of notice. We will provide em- ployees a minimum of 60 days written notice prior to their release date. Severance and completion bonus can only be earned by success- ful completion of assignment.

Q31   What rules govern when the severance is paid and can all or part of it be deferred until 1993? If employees work until their release date in mid- December, can they have their severance/bonus payout in January?

A31   Our basic policy is that all payouts are due upon termination. The IRS regulations regarding this are quite complex. We are continuing to re- view what alternatives, if any, exist.

Q33   Will most of our severance pay be lost in taxes?

A33   We are still exploring the taxation requirements for severance/comple- tion bonus payments.

Q46   If an employee is offered a job with an affiliate company but turns it down, will they still get severance and a completion bonus?

A46   Yes, provided they work until their release date.

Q49   When leaving do we get paid vacation for time accumulated only or do we get paid for the entire year's benefit?

A49   You will be paid vacation accrued up to termination date per Com- pany policy.

Q61   Can I receive my severance pay if I volunteer to leave prior to my scheduled release date if my services are no longer needed?

A61   At this point in time all employees should plan to work through their scheduled release date. It is possible as we get more insight into busi- ness requirements that some flexibility may be appropriate. We will handle these as they occur on a case-by-case basis consistent with business and legal requirements.

Q72   What deductions will be taken out of an individual's last check for PTO, vacation, severance and the completion bonus?

A72   None other than statutory taxes; i.e. state and federal taxes and FICA. All other deductions (insurance, ESP, etc.) will be taken only from wages earned through the last day worked.

Q83   How will the second severance pay be classified? (Bonus or severance.)

A83   For unemployment benefits, it will be classified as bonus.

Q96   If I was within 6 months of my anniversary date could there be a partial pay out?

A96   No. You must reach an anniversary date to be eligible for anniversary benefits. However, supervisors should take milestone dates into consideration in establishing final release dates.

Q98   What payroll deductions will be taken from the severance and the completion bonus?

A98   Only required taxes (FICA, Federal and State) will be taken from severance and completion bonuses. No other deductions will be taken.

Q100  Will all of the severance and completion bonus be on one check?

A100  Yes. The taxes would be the same if there is one or more checks.

Q115  Is overtime calculated into anything such as severance or pension?

A115  Overtime does count as "pension earnings" for figuring your "final average pay" under the pension plan. Severance is figured on your normal weekly rate (base rate plus shift differential) and does not include overtime.

Q120  Could I use vacation to carry my completion date into the next year? Since most of the people will have completion dates near the end of the year, additional severance and bonuses will hurt many due to taxes. Some may not stay for the completion because of the big hit on taxes?

A120  Release dates cannot be extended by use of vacation, PTO or severance.

Q125  If an employee works through their completion date here then transfers to another affiliate company do they still get their severance and completion bonus?

A125  No. An employee who accepts a *transfer* to another location and is not terminated as a RIF, will not be paid severance pay.

Q131  Will the company pay shift differential on severance, PTO and vacation accrual at plant closing?

A131  Yes, shift differential applies.

Q132  Will bonus vacations be paid, if not taken, at closing? Follow-up: Are they still being paid?

A132  Yes. Any unused vacation will be paid at the time you leave. Accruals for regular vacation are updated at the end of each month. Bonus vacation hours do not appear on your pay stub. They are tracked in Benefits and Payroll.

Q154 Will we receive a PTO payout before December?
A154 No.
Q163 Since the plant will be closing and there is the possibility of not being able to schedule vacation, why can't we be paid off our vacation hours now if we have earned it rather than when we leave the company?
A163 Unused vacation pay is payable upon termination. There is no provision for cashing in vacation or PTO pay.

## Job Opportunities

Q24 What about other company jobs?
A24 We will be contracting other site organizations to determine any interest they may have in our employees.
Q86 Did HR tell any employers not to hire plant employees until June 1992?
A86 No. Human Resources encourages any and all prospective employers to consider employees at any time. HR does advise them our formal in-house outplacement center will open in approximately June.
Q134 Could we get some New Mexico information for the employees interested in transferring, e.g., cost of living information, whether moving expenses will be paid, living expenses for first month, and anything else you might think of?
A134 Information is available in the HR office. If there is other information you may need, please let us know and we'll see what we can do.
Q143 Will there be transfers to off-shore sites and if so, how do they pay?
A143 Transfer to offshore locations are extremely unlikely due to immigration and work authorization legalities. Anyone who has a specific question should contact HR.

## Release Dates

Q7 When will the RIF's begin?
A7 Our precise closure schedule is not finalized. We would expect the ramp-down to begin at the end of Q3 in order to finish by year-end. Obviously business conditions will dictate how we proceed. How our customers will respond to this action is unclear so we will have to evaluate the situation on an ongoing basis.
Q17 If mutually agreed between employee and supervisor that employee is wasting time being at work, can requirements for notification and severance be waived?
A17 Scheduled release dates can be adjusted when business conditions support a change and some employees may be able to leave sooner. However, we are required to comply with the 60-day written notification requirements of the WARN Act.

Q19  Can an employee work after their release date for a business need?

A19  We can request that an employee work beyond their release date if mutually agreeable and it supports our business needs. It is purely voluntary on the employee's part, and a decision to not work past the release date will not affect the employee's eligibility for payment.

Q20  If we need an employee another week but he/she has a release date, are they free to leave on their release date?

A20  Yes.

Q21  Will employees forfeit their severance or completion bonus if they choose not to work the extra week?

A21  No.

Q22  In past layoffs we were able to take a voluntary RIF and still get severance. Why can't we now?

A22  This is a total plant closure as opposed to a small downsizing. We may be able to request volunteers first in some areas when release dates are finalized and when they support business plans. Severance pay is meant to be a financial bridge to a new job.

Q45  When areas close can employees with more seniority bump employees out of other areas?

A45  No. In order to provide an orderly closure, employees will leave as they complete their assignments. However, if an employee is needed for business reasons in another area, they may have a later release date, but they will not bump someone else.

Q50  What about MLOA's?

A50  Normal notification will be given by mail to anyone on medical leave whose release date occurs during the LOA. They will be RIF'd upon release from medical authority. Employees who return from MLOA who still have work available will be returned per policy.

Q52  Can employees switch release dates if they are in similar jobs?

A52  No. Individual release dates must be set for each employee and 60-day written notice provided. However, in the pre-planning of setting the original release date, supervisors may consider requests to be released earlier if it supports the business plans. Adjustments to release dates prior to the 60-day notification must be approved by he Department manager and Human Resources. We will try to take into account all personal wishes in assigning release dates to accommodate employees consistent with the business requirements.

Q54  Are there any kind of allowances for people who are near to completion of a bonus year anniversary?

A54  There are no special plans to deviate from normal eligibility rules. We will try to take circumstances like this into consideration in assigning release dates.

Q67  Can PTO or vacation be used to prolong employment past release dates?

A67 No. All employees will be paid all unused, accrued PTO and vacation pay on their release date.

Q81 Can I work part-time to my release date and still get severance and the completion bonus?

A81 Employees work schedules will be determined by department management. Employees should plan on working full-time through their release date. Exceptions, if any, must be reviewed by senior management and will be handled case-by-case.

Q97 Will exceptions be made for service adjustments that are within a certain time frame after I have my final completion date? This could make a difference in severance and pension.

A97 No. An employee's termination date is the last day worked. Supervisors should take into consideration milestone dates when establishing release dates for all their employees.

Q119 Will my seniority affect my release date?

A119 Release dates will be primarily a function of end of assignment. However, job skills, performance and seniority will be considered where a distinction is needed.

Q127 If we get more orders than we can possibly make before December 15, 1992, will we stay open long enough to make the parts or is December 15, 1992 the drop dead date and no work will be allowed after this date? Will the December 15 closure date be extended if goals are not met?

A127 The current plan is to close all production by December 15, 1992. If a change were to occur to this schedule, all affected employees would be notified.

Q128 If an operator has vacation scheduled and their release date falls in the middle of the vacation will they still get their severance and completion bonus?

A128 Unusual circumstances such as this will be considered case-by-case. Employee concerns including scheduled time off and eligibility for completion payments will be given every consideration.

Q149 Will Maintenance be kept around after the planned shutdown to help in closing down the plant and to help move equipment? A lot of Maintenance folks are interested in doing this and would like some information.

A149 There will be a number of personnel asked to remain beyond closure to provide cleanup service. We are currently working on our closure plan and its staffing implications. We expect to have a first cut of it within the next few months.


Relocation

Q8 How many people will be relocated?

A8 Specific numbers are not available. We intend to transfer some engineering functions to California and various process activities to other fab locations. This will of course provide opportunities for current plant employees. Other opportunities will also occur over time as a result of turnover and activities at other locations. These also could be a source of openings. Our Job Opportunity System will make such offsite opportunities available to you. It is our hope that any employee who wishes to relocate will have the opportunity to do so—but we can't be sure of that.

Q25  Will there be relocation benefits for SNE [salaried non-exempt] employees?

A25  All employees may be eligible for some relocation benefits for relocation within the company. the minimum benefit is a $1,200 flat allowance.

Q26  Will relocations take place all along or in the latter part of Quarter 3?

A26  The plans which will impact the timing of any relocations are being developed.

Q65  Will employees who receive a relocation offer be given an opportunity for a pre-move visit before final acceptance of the offer?

A65  In-plant area orientations will be provided several times during the closure process. All interested employees will have access to these. Company paid visits will be made available on a case-by-case basis. Any employee who wants to visit a company location should contact HR and we will assist with local contacts.

## Retirement

Q10  Will there be early retirement incentives available?

A10  No. Of course anyone who is eligible (or may become eligible during the closure period) can exercise his/her retirement options as they see fit. We have also made provisions to fully vest all employees reduced in force as a result of the closure. Thus any RIF'd employees with less than five years of service will have some benefits from our pension plan. The details of this are still being worked out and affected employees will be notified shortly. If you have any specific pension questions, please contact Benefits.

Q11  What will happen to my retirement funds?

A11  All retirement funds are protected through a trust and administered under complete legal compliance with ERISA [Employee Retirement Income Security Act]. Your pension fund will be available to you per normal qualification requirements.

Q27  Is early retirement possible?

A27  Yes, as early as age 55.

Q28  Will years of service be just at the plant or both company and plant years combined?

A28  For all purposes other than pension they are combined when no breaks in service occurred or if you were a RIF and returned within one year, or voluntarily quit and returned within 30 days. Past service is also credited once an employee has been continuously re-employed for six year. The crediting of past service for pension purposes follows a different set of rules. Contact benefits for more specific information.

Q36   Will we get calculations of our vested retirement and pension?

A36   Yes. Corporate human resources is working on the estimates now. We plan to provide them prior to an employee's scheduled release date.

Q58   How will a pension be calculated when an employee had service as both a salaried non-exempt and exempt? If the separate amounts are both less than $3499 but when added together over $3500, will they be paid out separately or in a lump sum?

A58   Pension benefits for non-exempt and exempt service are calculated separately. Eligibility for lump sum cash-outs is calculated separately for each piece. If the present value of one piece is less than $3500, that piece will be paid out as a lump sum. If the value of the other piece is also below $3500, it also will be paid out; if not, it will be paid as a monthly pension benefit at retirement.

Q59   How and when can we all find out how much is in our pension fund?

A59   There will be an initial distribution of current individual pension data on which calculations are based along with calculation information. This data will be available before the end of March. If there are any questions or concerns about this data, contact Benefits so that we can insure that all the data is accurate. A final estimate of pension benefits will be provided in advance of each employee's release date.

Q62   If your pension when calculated is less than $3500, will it be paid out in lump sum or retained at the employees option?

A62   If net present value of your pension is $3499 or less it will be paid out as a lump sum.

Q63   Does severance pay have to be used up before retirement benefits kick in?

A63   No. Severance is paid as a lump sum on your last day worked.

Q77   Who do you contact after the plant closure regarding benefit questions including retirement?

A77   A list of contacts will be provided as a handout prior to your release date.

Q84   For pensions over $3500, can an employee withdraw it?

A84   Under our pension plan provisions, pension amounts of $3500 or more must be left in the plan.

Q85   Can employees who retire still receive unemployment benefits?

A85   (Need to check EDD.) (In California, retirement payments are deducted from unemployment benefits but the difference, if any, is paid as long as the employee remains eligible.)

Q102  How and who would we contact in the future as to status of our pension?

A102   Contact the Benefits Department. On your release date we will provide you with a detailed list of contacts for such subjects as pension
and ESP.

Q103   What are the laws for pension payout? I understand that there is a law
that states an employer must pay out pension?

A103   ERISA requires, among other things, that employers provide pension
benefits to all "vested" employees. Normally at the company employees become vested after completing five years of pension eligibility service. As you know, we have waived the five year requirement
for plant employees, and all employees will be vested regardless of
service.

However, there is no law requiring companies to pay out pension in
a lump sum. The law allows companies to automatically pay benefits
in a lump sum if the present value of the pension is less than $3500,
but does not require it. The company has chosen to pay out pensions
of under $3500.

Q104   How were the amounts of $3499 or less determined? Who determines
the amount of lump sums?

A104   The law states that pensions of less than $3500 can be paid out as a
lump sum without the employee's consent. That's where the $3500
figure comes from. The law allows lump sum payment of a pension
based on the value that would provide for the most effective administration of pension funds. The plan established $3500 as that limit; that
is consistent with legal requirements.

The amount of lump sum pay out is determined by the "present
value" of the employee's pension. Present value is determined from
an actuarial table, established by an independent actuarial firm, in accordance with accepted accounting principles.

"Present value" is the lump sum amount that, if invested at termination with a reasonable rate of interest and left untouched until age 65,
would be enough to pay an amount equal to the employee's monthly
pension benefit for his or her lifetime, starting at age 65. For example, if
the monthly pension benefit is $100 per month and the employee is age
38 at termination, present value is the amount that would have to be
invested now to pay $100 per month, beginning in 27 years. The youn-
ger the employee is at termination, the smaller the present value will be,
because there are more years for interest to accumulate. So, the variables
that go into the determination are the employee's age at termination and
the amount of his/her monthly pension benefit.

Q105   How are lump sums calculated?

A105   When an employee terminates, we calculate a monthly pension benefit based on the employee's age. We multiply the monthly pension
benefit by the factor. If the product is less than $3500, the employee
gets a lump sum pay out. If it is more than $3500, the pension is paid
as a monthly benefit at retirement. The younger the employee and the

smaller the monthly pension, the greater likelihood that the employee will receive a lump sum pay out.

Q106    What if you die and have not received your pension or your pay out?

A106    If you are married, the pension plan contains provisions to pay benefits to your spouse if you die before your pension begins. If you are to receive a lump sum, it would be paid to your spouse. If your pension is deferred until retirement, your spouse will automatically be covered by a "Pre-Retirement Surviving Spouse" option, unless you reject it. If your pension is deferred, you will receive more information regarding surviving spouse benefits when you leave the company.

If you are single and die before pension benefits are paid, no benefits are payable to anyone else.

Q107    Can I get a pension pay out later? Can we sign a pension lump sum waiver and not receive the amount now? What law exists?

A107    No. Eligibility for a lump sum pay out is determined at termination. Employees do not have the option to defer pay out, or to request pay out at a later date. If your pensions's present value is less than $3500, you will receive a lump sum pay out.

Q108    How soon will I get my pension estimate?

A108    Initial pension data forms, showing you the information that will be used to calculate your benefit, will be available by the end of March. As soon as completion dates are known, estimates will be prepared for employees in order of completion dates.

Q109    If I do not receive a pension lump sum will it earn interest until I apply for retirement?

A109    The pension plan pays a defined benefit. You will know when you leave the company what your monthly pension will be at retirement. The monthly benefit amount does not increase in value by earning interest.

Q110    Can pension lump sums be rolled over to avoid taxes?

A110    Yes, if appropriate IRA guidelines are followed.

Q123    Operators know other operators that, in the past, have pulled out all their pension fund as one lump sum even though it was more than $3500. If so, why can't we do the same thing now, especially since the closure is not our option?

A123    Employees who may have had two pension plans, one non-exempt and one exempt, both of which were less than $3500 may have received a combined amount over $3500.

Q124    Does the pension plan allow us to pay anyone a lump sum when the pension is $3500 or more?

A124    No. The company pension plan as qualified under federal regulation restricts this.

Q155    Is it possible to receive a partial $3500 retirement payout and keep the rest in the retirement fund if your retirement fund is greater than $3500?

A155    No.

Q158    What is the answer to the question on medical insurance for retirees? Can any special concern be given for those not age 65 who must take a reduction if they retire now?

A158    We have submitted a request to Corporate to review this request. Once a decision is made we will communicate it.

Q161    Can we leave our pension to anyone else than our spouse?

A161    No.

Q162    Is pension federally or state regulated?

A162    It's a federally qualified plan.


## Training/Outplacement

Q6    Will the company provide for any retraining?

A6    The company has expressed a willingness to fund a retraining effort through the Utah Employment Development Department. We are still working out the details of this and as soon as they are available we will let you know.

Q37    What about retraining funds?

A37    We are working with the State to determine an appropriate retraining program. We have indicated a willingness to fund such a program.

Q38    Is that funding for retraining voluntary on the company's part?

A38    Yes.

Q39    Will education benefits, i.e. tuition reimbursement, continue?

A39    Yes, provided you work until your release date which falls after the class begins or the class is completed prior to your voluntary termination and provided the benefits are otherwise payable under our policy.

Q40    When will retraining begin?

A40    We are currently working with State officials on developing retraining plans. They will be announced as they are finalized.

Q41    It would be helpful to start outplacement procedures early because of sale of houses, etc. Can we do that?

A41    Current plan is to begin formal outplacement activities in the plant two months prior to the commencement of formal downsizing. Approximately June 92. We are exploring some preliminary training earlier than that.

Q51    Will WordPerfect classes be offered as part of retraining?

A51    To be determined as retraining plan is developed.

Q53    Has the company reapplied for assistance through the Trade Adjustment Act?

A53    We are currently discussing training opportunities with State officials.

Q64    When is the latest date an employee can sign up for tuition reimbursement?

A64    The approved course must start prior to your release date. Employees who voluntarily quit prior to their release date and have not completed a course, will forfeit a tuition reimbursement payment. All courses must be concluded by the end of the 1992 fall term.

Q87   What is being done to gain training benefits under the Trade Adjustment Act?

A87   We are currently preparing and filing a petition with the U.S. Department of Labor, under the Trade Act of 1972, and Trade Adjustment Assistance Act therein for training funds eligibility. The process time for filing such a petition and receiving a response from the Labor Department is 60 to 90 days.

Q88   Will more than two courses be allowed for the tuition reimbursement program?

A88   The tuition reimbursement policy remains unchanged and the maximum is two courses per term.

Q89   Will you cover adult education courses such as English, computer classes, WordPerfect? Are classes outside of a technical or business related major now allowed?

A89   We will continue to support those business-related courses we have approved in the past. All classes outside the normal tuition reimbursement plan will be evaluated as part of our retraining plan.

Q90   Will the educational scholarship program continue for previous winners? Will it continue for the plant this year?

A90   Yes, once company scholarships are awarded, they continue for the four years of undergraduate study, regardless of whether the parent remains with the company. The 1992 scholarship program will be available for the children who are currently high school seniors, as long as the parent is employed on May 1, 1992.

Q136  Is the plant closure not being classified as due to foreign competition and therefore governmental retraining benefits will not be available?

A136  No. We have applied for retraining funding through the Department of Labor.

Q137  Will there be funds to continue training for programs you are currently enrolled in?

A137  Yes. The normal educational reimbursement program will continue until the closure is complete. Employees enrolled in an approved class prior to his/her release date, will be eligible for reimbursement for that class.

Q140  If a person has a degree, are they eligible for TRA benefits? Will current classes go towards TRA training?

A140  Eligibility criteria are set and administered by the TRA people. There may be restrictions. Once the Labor Department makes a decision on our eligibility for TRA benefits, eligibility requirements currently in affect will be shared. We will continue to research this question.

Q142  What type of retraining classes will be provided for production workers and when would they be offered. Will we be able to leave production for any on-site training?

A142    Information on retraining options will be available shortly. The plan is to schedule these classes during non-work hours to accommodate all shifts.

Q146    In reference to classes/retraining that the company is offering due to the shutdown, will the company require non-exempts to take PTO/vacation for the time they are not on-site?

A146    It is anticipated that retraining classes will be identified during non-working hours. If an employee is approved for a class during the normal work day, they will be required to take PTO, vacation or unpaid time if it does not conflict with the business plan.

Q147    If non-exempts must take the time off of their time cards for off-site classes, shouldn't the rule be the same for exempts?

A147    Rules governing non-exempts and exempts are not the same. Non-exempts are paid overtime and exempts are required to work hours necessary to accomplish their assigned tasks. But once again, it is our intent to schedule training to the maximum extent possible during non-working time.


## Unemployment

Q34    How will severance, vacation and PTO payouts affect unemployment?

A34    Unemployment benefits are affected only by payments for vacation and initial severance/or pay in lieu of notice. Other kinds of payments, such as second severance (or completion bonus), should not affect the start date of your unemployment benefits. Representatives from Job Service will be invited to the plant in approximately June 92 to discuss eligibility, the filing process and to answer any specific questions on unemployment settlements. Employees are, of course, free to contact Job Service at any time.

Q48    How long do unemployment benefits last?

A48    Normally 26 weeks, but employees should check with Job Service. Again, Job Service will be on site during this process to discuss benefits in approximately June 92.

Q57    When can I start collecting unemployment?

A57    Job Service will be invited in to answer questions on their program as part of our outplacement service. Individuals can contact Job Service earlier if they need information immediately.

Q60    How will severance pay or a completion bonus be treated by Job Service as it related to my unemployment benefits?

A60    See Q34.

Q95    Will anniversary bonus and bonus pay affect the start date for unemployment?

A95    No. However, regular severance and vacation will affect the start date of unemployment.

Q101    What is the maximum amount of unemployment?

A101    Job Service will be invited into the facility prior to your release date to answer all unemployment questions. Should an employee wish, they can contact Job Service at any time.

Q141    Will unemployment be extended if you are going through a training program?

A141    It may be possible that some programs for which we have applied may provide extended unemployment benefits. The details of these programs will be announced as we receive them.


## General

Q1    This decision has been a long time in the making. Why didn't you tell us sooner?

A1    In actual fact, the basic decision was not made until the week of December 16. Once that happened, a number of sub-decisions needed to be made—some of which are still not concluded. We wanted to give you as much information as possible in a timely and orderly way. We have given you the information as quickly as we could. Additionally, final closure is some time away giving each of us ample time to work problems and concerns.

Q2    Will we still get a focal point? If so, why?

A2    We will be announcing our 1992 compensation program shortly. It is currently planned to provide a focal point increase at all locations, including Utah. The issues the company faces are not solved by delaying or stopping pay increases—they are product line and organization issues that require more focused changes. We still intend to pay our people competitively for however long they are here and to recognize past contributions and future efforts.

Q79    Will 1992 focal points be given?

A79    Yes, per normal process.

Q3    What about legal warning requirements?

A3    We believe we are in full compliance with all statutory regulations regarding notice to individuals affected as well as to local and government agencies. We intend to remain in compliance.

Q9    Do we have specific shutdown schedules?

A9    In order to close the facility by year-end the ramp down must start by the end of September. There may be some interim work force adjustments but this will be dictated by business needs and how customers react to this decision.

Q12    I thought the Utah plant was profitable and the New Mexico plant was not. Why did you pick Utah?

A12    The New Mexico plant was "unprofitable" largely because of under-utilized capacity. That underutilized capacity is very modern. In rationalizing our capacity requirements, it only makes sense to close the least modern operation—in this case it is the Utah plant.

Q13    Why all the facility work if we are closing?

A13    We still need to operate for the remainder of this year and our commitment to worker's safety remains unchanged. Thus we have done facility work—and will continue to do more during the remainder of the year—to ensure viable operations and safe occupancy. Of course we hope that the building is attractive to another occupant after we close and it is only wise to maintain it in good shape.

Q15    If we are pruning these products, what are the implications on Korea and/or Bangkok?

A15    Obviously there will be impacts but precisely what kind are not clear yet. We need to finalize our product plans/portfolio and also we need to understand our customer's reactions to these decisions.

Q23    Where will our plant assets go?

A23    If equipment can be used it will be transferred to a new location. Items of high value will be put up for sale to the public/business. There may be an employee sale toward to the end of the plant closure. More details of this will be made available as we get closer to the closure.

Q29    What is happening with Fab 1?

A29    Fab 1 continues to operate and will operate as long as their product portfolio and effectiveness allows.

Q32    With regard to the Plant Staff daily/weekly meetings, how often will we hear back from you?

A32    Managers of each department will determine the best way to pass information along.

Q44    Can we have supervisor/manager meetings on all shifts?

A44    Yes.

Q47    Referring to the letter going out to all employees, should the original or copy be returned to human resources?

A47    We prefer the employee keep the original letter and return the copy with their signature. The signature denotes receipt. If the employee does not want to sign the letter, the supervisor needs to send back the copy stating they gave the letter to the employee and the date.

Q55    Will the Credit Union still exist after the plant closure?

A55    Yes, they will move offsite to a location yet to be determined.

Q66    Can employees be given letters of recommendation?

A66    Because of various legal and statutory complications, there will be no letters of recommendation provided on Company letterhead. This does not preclude individual supervisors/managers providing their own personal statement.

All employees will receive on Company letterhead a letter announcing the plant closure.

Q68   What about any overtime?

A68   This is determined by the level of business and general manning needs.

Q70   Will ERT bonus compensation still be paid?

A70   If you are an ERT and remain actively in this capacity through your release date you will be eligible for any benefits for ERT members.

Q74   How long will the Company Store remain open?

A74   Through the summer. The exact closure date has not yet been determined.

Q80   Will normal promotions be considered?

A80   Yes, per normal qualification requirements.

Q99   What is the maximum number of tax deductions I can use?

A99   There is no limit on the number of deductions allowed. However, ten or more deductions must be reported to the IRS.

Q116  Do employees need to turn in their Employee Handbook when they leave?

A116  No, the handbook is yours to keep. Company property, such as manuals, will need to be returned.

Q129  Will we still need to do RMO's for the rest of 1992? If so, why? (Please be specific and do not say "Business as usual.")

A129  We need to establish RMO's in order to establish clear goals toward which the employees can best and efficiently support our business plans.

Q133  Could employees attend the SOS meeting?

A133  The Company has no objection to anyone attending citizen meetings of any kind. The SOS organization sets meeting requirements and employees are free to contact them to see what they may require. Attendance would not be paid time other than vacation or PTO.

Q135  Could we get weekly meetings scheduled to keep the rumor mill at a tolerable level?

A135  Normal monthly all-employee communications meetings are being planned in addition to monthly area meetings. Additionally, periodic all supervisor/manager meetings are being planned. The most important communication linkage is supervisor/employee. Please don't wait for meetings to get your questions asked. All our supervisors are happy to deal with them as they occur.

Q138  Since we are closing can the smokers come inside?

A138  No. We are still maintaining a smoke-free environment per current policy?

Q139  Will Utah employees be disqualified from participation in "Life After TIP" due to forced termination prior to year end?

A139  At this point in time there has been no decision on any 1992 additional compensation plans. If such a plan is provided, eligibility for it will be announced at that time. We must recognize the fact that the plant's situation is unique and may require other than normal handling.

Q144  Can we copy EP's for employees?
A144  Yes.
Q150  Is the New Mexico Plant being sold to M.E.C.?
A150  No.
Q151  Is Intel buying us?
A151  No.
Q152  Is there any possibility to have access to Personnel on the graveyard shift for individual needs?
A152  The Benefits Department is here everyday at 6:30 a.m. If there are other needs, your DHR can make special arrangements.
Q153  Will we have an employee sale? If so, when?
A153  First sale on excess non-redeployable assets will be in late March 92. An announcement will be made on the specific items to be included. Future employee sales will be announced when appropriate.

# Appendix 2: Worker Adjustment Information Packet

### Being Out of Work Doesn't Mean Being Out of Opportunities

#### Introduction

Unemployment, the loss of one's job, affects individuals both emotionally and financially. Typically, the reduction of income is the first noticeable change in the household. As the period of unemployment lengthens, the emotional impact and the resulting stress become greater burdens. Together these factors can damage otherwise stable family or personal relationships. Understanding and taking immediate action to control these negative effects of unemployment are the focus of the "Dislocated Worker Workshop."

#### Take Immediate Action

Taking immediate action will require adequate planning if you are to be successful. This planning should be based on thorough investigation and self-evaluation. It should be done along with those persons having the greatest knowledge of your situation or those who will be most affected by these decisions. Much of the planning and decision-making, however, will be done by you. Be sure to take enough time to think and collect information. Try to find a quiet place where you will not be disturbed by others.

*Plan a Budget*

As soon as you learn of a layoff or termination, you should quickly face the financial realities of your job loss. Your income will be lower. By developing budgetary plans early, you can forestall or avoid completely more severe spending reductions later. Once your spending plans are in place, you will be free to concentrate on your job search activities. Furthermore, taking these actions may help reduce anxiety and stress.

When preparing a budget, the following items must be considered:

1. Cash on hand
2. Monthly living expenses
3. Sources of income
4. Job search expenses

Identify where your money is going. Measure your needs versus your wants. Prioritize your expenses, giving serious consideration to the basic necessities; mortgage or rent payments, utilities, property taxes, food, health care and transportation expenses. At the first sign of job loss, reduce or eliminate expenses for items that you want, but do not need, e.g., entertainment, new clothing, VCR, etc. Ask yourself "will I need this item within the next three days?" If not this will give you three days to decide whether you need it at all. Do not take on any new debts unless absolutely necessary.

*Plan Daily Accomplishments*

When the structure of the work environment is removed, it is all too easy to "fritter" away your time. By planning goals in your daily schedule, you will be less likely to harm your self-esteem. As you complete each task, check it off your list. Such routines organize your days and make you aware of your accomplishments.

*Plan Your Job Search*

Of course, the best way to cope with unemployment is to find another job as soon as possible. Planning and implementing an effective job search takes sustained effort. It is not a quick-fix venture. Job seeking activities should be the major focus of your daily activities. *Your new job is finding a job.*

If you have not looked for work for some time, your job search skills may be a little rusty! Many books and pamphlets on resume preparation and job search are available through libraries or your local Job Service Office. If you are having difficulty finding work on your own, you may get help through your local Job Training Partnership Act, Title III Economic Dislocation and Worker Adjustment Assistance Act (EDWAA). Locations of these offices are found on page 2 of the pink section of this packet.

Let your friends and colleagues know you are seeking employment—but be specific about your job target. The more clearly you can describe your own goals, the easier it will be for others to identify possible job leads for you. People are more likely to help you in your employment search if you provide them with an up-to-date copy or your resume. Many people find job openings through personal contacts and friends, so don't limit the scope of your job search by keeping quiet.

Try to increase your number of business contacts. A good way to make contacts is by attending trade or professional association functions. You may also find out about job openings that will never be advertised. Also, you will be recognized by people who are aware of openings or are hiring. But again, sustained effort is needed to keep in contact with these people between meetings. These same business contacts can supply helpful information about a company's policies and business philosophy prior to an interview, so you will be prepared, informed and confident.

Finally, you must persevere. Follow up on all job leads. Call back after the interview and again later if someone else is hired for the job. In some cases, the person hired may not be suited to the position and may be discharged or will leave soon after being hired. Perhaps you were the second person under consideration or maybe an additional position has opened up. If the person doing the hiring has you fresh in his/her memory, your chances of landing the job are greatly increased.

## Understanding Reactions to Job Loss

Although our jobs provide us with money and thereby a particular standard of living, they also make us feel productive and useful—ourselves, our families and society. Our jobs give a sense of belonging and contributing to a group—whether it be our work unit, company or union. Frequently, when we are asked about who we are, we describe ourselves in terms of our work e.g., "I'm a fire fighter"; "I work for the LDS Hospital as a nurse." Thus our identities and self-respect are dependent on our jobs to a great extent. The sudden loss of employment causes disruptions in our lives, reorders our priorities (both personal and financial), and damages our self-esteem. Many people are not adequately prepared to handle the stress of unemployment. They are unable to deal with the emotional stress upon family relationships and friendships or the anxiety of possibly relocating to a new area.

Like all major changes in our lives, the fear of the "unknown" is a substantial hurdle in coping with unemployment. When we lose our job, we may experience a loss similar to a death of a close friend or relative. And, although the degree of emotional loss may be less, most of us will experience a similar grieving process. The Continuum Center of Oakland University has identified the typical stages of grief following job loss. Read through the descriptions below. If you find you are "stuck" in one stage, you may want to talk to someone, perhaps even a professional counselor, about your feelings.

*Stage 1. Happiness or Shock and Denial*
Some people at first feel wonderful—happy at having a "vacation" or relief that the waiting is over. For most of us there is a numbness. We don't believe that we really have lost our job, we hope for a recall when this is very unlikely. We don't act, because we do not really accept our loss.

*Stage 2. Emotion Release*
We need to vent our feelings or anger, sadness, frustration, jealously, etc. Holding in feelings may lead to physical symptoms or may delay moving on to action.

*Stage 3. Depression and Physical Distress*
We feel lost and helpless. We doubt our abilities. We may feel hopelessness. We experience physical signs of stress like sleepiness, loss of appetite or back and stomach problems.

*Stage 4. Panic and Guilt*

We have trouble thinking clearly and cannot plan effectively. We feel responsible for the layoff even though we had no control over it. We keep thinking, "if only." We try to do everything at once and do nothing efficiently.

*Stage 5. Anger and Hostility*

This is an important part of the recovery process. Anger can be positive, but we feel angry at those around us. We need to learn to use these strong feelings to give us the energy to make plans and move on to the next stage.

*Stage 6. Renewed Hope and Rebuilding*

We begin to plan for our new life without the old job. We are able to take constructive action toward obtaining a new job.

*Stage 7. Resolution*

We let go of our anger and false hopes. We feel in control or our lives again. The loss is still part of us but does not dictate our actions.

## Dealing with Stress

*Stress*

Stress is the body's response to demands made upon it. Change is a primary cause of stress. Unemployment forces make changes upon our established routines, spending patterns, and aspirations. Not only is our source of income gone, but so is our daily structure, the social interaction of the job and, most importantly, our sense of purpose. And as time goes on, our self-esteem and sense of value may diminish. But keep in mind that, although we may be feeling disorganized or not in control, there are many things we can do to relieve our anxiety and diffuse stress.

*Communication*

Communication with others is the key element in reducing stress. Isolation can block our progress to becoming reeemployed. Continued social isolation may lead to depression. Any problem is easier to handle if we share it with someone who is concerned. our problems can be put into perspective when we know people care about us, but they cannot provide help and understanding if they are unaware of our feelings and concerns.

It is not easy to ask for help when you are "down," but often this is the time when you need help most. If friends or relatives are unavailable, then you should seek out others who are, such as previous co-workers, clergy, or neighbors. If serious problems arise, professional counseling should be considered.

*Exercise*

Exercise is an effective way to work off tension. Some form of daily exercise is essential to your physical and emotional well being, wether you choose walking, biking, aerobics, or running.

Team or group sports like softball or bowling provide both exercise and social interaction. When confronted with budget considerations, be sure not to shortchange yourself where sensible, low-cost recreation is concerned. In the long run it is money well spent. Exercise and healthy competition combined with the attainment of personal physical goals can bolster your bruised self-esteem and enhance your sense of accomplishment. They will leave you renewed and refreshed to face your daily challenges.

*Helping Others*

Helping others is another means of raising your self-esteem. This can be done in many different ways. Some people use this period of unemployment to establish close relationships with family members. One study suggests that, although increased stress is handled successfully, there may actually be improved communication between family members. Sometimes you are able to acquire a greater understanding of your family members' abilities and contributions. This may be a time when family activities can be planned and shared together—whether it is a household project or short trip.

Volunteer activities can be rewarding and worthwhile. You may be able to upgrade certain job related skills through volunteer experience. Keep in mind that " your new job is finding a job." Make sure that your volunteer time does not interfere with your job search activities.

## Identifying Resources

Much of your concern during periods of unemployment will focus on financial needs. During this time of reduced income, you should make use of all financial assistance and counseling (career or personal) resources. This Workshop today will present a number of assistance programs and resources which are available to you. You will learn that BEING OUT OF WORK DOES NOT MEAN BEING OUT OF OPPORTUNITIES. Actually you will see that being a dislocated worker can provide you with opportunities that otherwise you may never have had—they are yours, take advantage of them.

# Appendix 3:
## Formal Closure Correspondence

Employee Release Date Letter

October 9, 1992

Dear

As indicated in your _____ Plant Closure letter, dated January 16, 1992, your separation date is dependent upon your particular job assignment and once determined you would receive prompt notice. Your individual separation date has been determined and in accordance with the Workers Adjustment and Retraining Notification Act, this letter is to advise that you will be permanently separated from [company] on December 18, 1992.

Thank you for your continued support and your commitment to do your best in assisting in a very difficult and necessary decision.

If you have any questions regarding this letter, please contact me at extension _____.

Sincerely,

Human Resource Manager

_____          _____

Employee Signature                Date                 Badge #

Retention Bonus Letter

January 20, 1992

Re: _____ Plant Closure

As you are aware, on January 15, 1992 we announced the decision to permanently close the _____ facility. While the exact date is not yet determined, we anticipate closure by the end of 1992.

You possess certain management/technical skills which are critical to the orderly plant closure program. We recognize the value of your skills and offer you the following to help us ensure the effective closure and transfer of activities.

Your separation date is dependent upon your particular job assignment, but we do not expect the rampdown to start in earnest until mid to end of Quarter 3. Upon completion of your assignment every consideration for an appropriate available position elsewhere in the Company will be provided. However, you will not be considered for another position within the _____ plant unless business requirements exist. While placement efforts will be made on your behalf it is possible no other assignment will be available. In that case, you will be permanently separated from _____. As soon as your individual situation is known, you will be given at least sixty (60) days notice of your scheduled termination date.

If separation is necessary you will receive any earned PTO and/or vacation you are entitled to under _____ policy. In addition, if you remain continuously employed and successfully complete your assignment and placement within _____ is not secured, in addition to normal severance pay you will receive an amount equivalent to _____ months salary as a completion bonus. This completion bonus applies only to your current assignment and is not transferable. The terms of this agreement are to be treated in a confidential manner and not discussed with other employees.

We ask that you continue to provide the effort and dedication necessary to bring this unfortunate but necessary task to its successful conclusion. Thank you for your continued support and your commitment to do your best in assisting in a very difficult and necessary decision.

If you have any questions regarding this letter, please contact your supervisor and/or your Division Human Resource Manager,

_____        _____

**EMPLOYEE**                    **DATE**                    **COMPANY**

# References

Berenbeim, R. *Company Programs to Ease the Impact of Shutdowns.* Report, no. 878. New York: Conference Board.

Blinder, A. S. 1988. Plant Closings: It Pays to Give Workers Advance Notice. *Business Week,* 6 June: 19.

Bluestone, Barry, and Bennett Harrison. 1982. *The Deindustrialization of America: Plant Closings, Community Abandonment, and the Dismantling of Basic Industry.* New York: Basic Books.

Bureau of National Affairs. 1985. *Plant Closings: The Complete Resource Guide.* Washington, D.C. BNA.

Engel, P. G. 1986. Plant Closings: Informing the Troops. *Industry Week* 231, 13 October: 33.

Eves, J. H., Jr. 1985. When a Plant Shuts Down: Easing the Pain. *Personnel* 62, 2 (February): 16–23.

Feldman, D. 1988. Helping Displaced Workers: The UAW-GM Human Resource Center. *Personnel* 65 (March): 34.

Franzem, J. J. 1987. Easing the Pain. *Personnel Administrator* 32 (February): 48–55.

Kinicki, A., et al. 1987. Socially Responsible Plant Closings. *Personnel Administrator* 32, 6 (June): 116–28.

Leana, C. R., and D. C. Feldman. 1988. Layoffs: How Employees and Companies Cope. *Personnel Journal* 67 (September): 31.

Perkins, D. S. 1987. What Can CEOs Do for Displaced Workers? *Harvard Business Review* 65 (November-December 1987): 90–93.

Portz, John. 1990. *The Politics of Plant Closings.* Lawrence, Kans.: University Press of Kansas.

Rothstein, L. E. 1986. *Plant Closings: The Roles of Myth, Power, and Politics.* Dover, Mass.: Auburn House.

Schippani, M. 1987. Creative Alternatives to Plant Closings: The Massachusetts Experience. *Labor Law Journal* 38, 8 (August): 460–64.

Sculnick, M. W. 1987. Plant Closings and Mass Layoffs—Toward a Cooperative Approach. *Employment Relations Today* 14, 2 (Summer 1987): 99–106.

Staudohar, P. D., and H. E. Brown. 1987. *Deindustrialization and Plant Closure.* Toronto: Lexington Books.

Targ, H. R., et al. 1988. Worker Responses to Plant Closings. *Labor Law Journal* 39, 8 (August): 562–66.

U.S. Department of Labor, Bureau of Labor-Management Relations and Co-operative Programs. 1990. *Plant Closing Checklist: A Guide to Best Practice.* BLMR 107. Washington, D.C.

# Index